Ching's
Fast Food

110 Quick and Healthy
Chinese Favourites

Ching's
Fast Food

110 Quick and Healthy Chinese Favourites

CHING-HE HUANG

HarperCollins*Publishers*

For all my family, friends, fans and 'gue-ren', thank you so much from my heart. A little bit more of me to you, with love.

First published in 2011 by Collins
an imprint of HarperCollins*Publishers*
77–85 Fulham Palace Road
London W6 8JB

www.harpercollins.co.uk

10 9 8 7 6 5 4 3 2 1

Photography © Jamie Cho 2011
Text, food and styling © Ching-He Huang 2011

Ching-He Huang asserts her moral right to be identified as the author of this work.

A catalogue record for this book is available from the British Library.

ISBN: 978-0-00-742627-0

Editorial: Georgina Atsiaris and Kate Parker
Design: Sophie Martin and Joanna MacGregor
Colour reproduction, printing and binding by Butler Tanner & Dennis Ltd, Frome

introduction   6

Breakfast   14

Soups   26

Appetisers   38

Chicken & Duck   74

Beef, Pork & Lamb   96

Fish & Shellfish   118

Vegetarian   140

Specials   158

Rice   180

Noodles   192

Dessert   206

equipment   222
glossary   228
index   236
acknowledgements   240

Introduction

Enough is enough.

Chinese food doesn't get the recognition it rightly deserves in the Western world. French, Japanese, even Korean cuisine all receive high praise from food critics in the press, but Chinese food remains underappreciated. Chinese cuisine can be just as complex or as basic as any other cuisine. It has so much to offer and has given so much already. It has travelled all over the world with immigrant Chinese families and its influence can be seen in the food cultures of many different countries, from Asia – Japan, Thailand and Vietnam – to Indonesia and the West.

Did you know that there are more takeaway Chinese restaurants in America than every McDonald's, Burger King and KFC put together? In the UK there are more than 15,000 Chinese takeaways and restaurants, and Chinese takeaways have officially overtaken Indian takeaways as the nation's favourite type of meal to order in every week. In America, Chinese restaurants first developed to provide food for the railway workers in the 19th century. Immigrant chefs had to use local ingredients to cater for their customers' tastes, so dishes were given a name and number and served with a very un-Chinese roll and butter. These were the circumstances in which Chinese takeaway menus were first devised.

During this period and over the years, many inventive takeaway dishes were created, including egg foo yung (omelette served with gravy), chow mein (stir-fried noodles), chop suey (leftovers in a brown sauce), crispy beef and General Tso's chicken (battered chicken in a spicy sweet ketchup sauce) – dishes as well loved in Britain and America as shepherd's pie, or steak and chips.

If you are a fan of your local Chinese takeaway and you then travel to China, my guess is that you will experience more than a culture shock, for the food will seem very unfamiliar. Some English businessmen have admitted to me that they fill their suitcases with crisps and other goodies when they travel to China because they cannot stomach the food there! If you go with an open mind, however, you'll discover a whole new culinary world. Should you be lucky enough to dine with Chinese friends at their favourite Chinese haunt, you'll find the menu will be dismissed, there will be a few exchanges of Cantonese or Mandarin, some quick scribbles by the waiter and you'll be treated to such delicacies as clay pot chicken, braised chicken's feet, 'fish-fragrant' aubergine, steamed sea cucumbers and baked salted chicken.

But there are signs that the disparity between takeaway food and 'real' Chinese cuisine is lessening. China has opened up over the last decade and there are now many more opportunities for travel to and from the country. The internet has helped too. As a result, more people are beginning to appreciate that Chinese cooking is much more than what is served at their local takeaway.

Chinese takeaway food has also recently moved on and become more exciting. There are more dim sum restaurants than ever, for instance, and while Cantonese cuisine is still the most widely served outside China, establishments offering dishes from other regions are sprouting up all over the place – no longer just Cantonese, but Sichuanese, Hunanese, Taiwanese and Shanghainese. Chinese takeaway food remains a huge phenomenon. Chinese takeaways can be found all over the world and each one has a unique story attached to it. Often you will hear how someone's grandfather started the takeaway, or how the place has been in the same family for generations. By contrast, others have changed ownership many times, serving as a golden goose for perhaps a decade before being passed on.

When my family first arrived in England and we stood waiting for a train, I remember an elderly couple asking my father whether we owned a takeaway or Chinese restaurant. That was two decades ago when it was the norm for newly arrived Chinese families to open a takeaway. The majority of my father's friends in the Chinese community in London owned takeaways.

In hindsight, my father thought he probably would have been more successful had he followed suit rather than going into the import–export business. At the time, however, he felt this was the right thing to do, as my grandparents were proud that their eldest son had graduated with a business degree and were prejudiced against him working in catering, which was considered laborious and low skilled (still the view in China today).

My first takeaway experience was in England – at a small place on the Fortune Green Road in North London. Prior to that I had never had food from one. My mother is a great cook, and when we lived in South Africa (before travelling to England), she made all the meals. Her recipes were mainly Chinese but with a South African twist, such as a stir-fried or traditional stewed dish served with miele pap (rather like polenta) instead of boiled rice.

In fact, there were no Chinese takeaways that I can recall during my time in South Africa. There was only one Chinese supermarket in Jo'burg at the time, which my mum would religiously frequent every week to stock up on provisions for her Chinese larder.

In England, by contrast, there were a lot more takeaways and one busy weekday, shortly after we had arrived in the country, we ordered from our local. The experience wasn't too bad, but Mum found it overly expensive and the fried rice not up to standard, so she turned her nose up at it and we never ordered from there again. The takeaway remains in business, however: last time I passed, it was still there. Mum preferred the Cantonese restaurant, the Water Margin, on Golders Green Road, and we went there when she wasn't in the mood for cooking. The restaurant became the place where I could meet my friends (or a date) for a quick Saturday lunch while satisfying my craving for Cantonese roast duck on rice.

Chinese takeaways are the 'fast food' of Chinese cuisine. A takeaway is where you would go to get your fried spring rolls, fried wontons, special fried rice or beef with greens. It is usually a lot more salty and oily than home-cooked Chinese food, in which dishes are a lot simpler, less rich and better balanced. It is no wonder that Chinese takeaways have created a bad name for themselves with many using high levels of monosodium glutamate to enhance the flavour. Although MSG is a natural substance, found in many foodstuffs, used as an additive it can have adverse effects. I personally have an intolerance to it, suffering from heart palpitations and a dry throat.

To me, if you use the freshest ingredients, you don't need MSG because the dish will be full of flavour, especially if those ingredients are in season and at their very best. Many manufacturers of Chinese or Asian condiments often add MSG, and I have found that a small amount within a sauce is fine, but commercial sauces can contain quite a bit. Try and find ones that don't have MSG and contain ingredients that are as natural as possible. Best of all, create your own sauces – in this book I'll show you how to use store-cupboard ingredients to make your own. It is true of all cuisines that the foods you cook yourself at home will be healthier and lighter than any takeaway food. In fact, a recent report showed that a meal cooked at home contains on average 1,000 fewer calories than its takeaway/restaurant equivalent and considerably less salt. Even though my grandmother was partial to a little 'gourmet powder' (MSG) from time to time, she always practised what she preached – to be certain of what you're eating, it is better to cook the food yourself.

That's not to say that I'm not partial to a Chinese takeaway myself; indeed, there is a good one near where I live in North West London. I happen to know the owner and have been to the factory where the special 11-spice powder they use for their crispy aromatic duck is lovingly ground, and it's so good! When I don't have anything in my fridge or want to give myself time off in the kitchen, I just give them a ring and order number 15. But unless you know the establishment well, it's like takeaway roulette, and we've all had a bad takeaway experience at some time or another. If you have a reliable local takeaway, support the owners and treat them like family!

I actually love Chinese food in all its forms – Americanised, anglicised, even bastardised. I recently had the pleasure of trying Chinese chicken salad American-style and I could see the attraction in the sweet orange sauce coupled with crispy fried wonton skins, crunchy lettuce and chicken strips. Yes, God forbid, I have even had a craving for it since! (I blame it entirely on the sugary sauce.) There is beauty in Chinese takeaway food that is cooked well – even a pretty standard dish like sweet and sour pork balls. I know some expats living Hong Kong who demand to have some of the anglicised takeaway stuff and would import it if they could. It is simply a matter of taste. And what most fascinates me is how thousands of people all over the world are united in their love of Chinese takeaway food, while the forefathers of this invention were completely unaware that they were the pioneers of Chinese fast food and the very best in their field. It is an amazing achievement when you think about it: these days R&D (research and development) chefs get paid six-figure sums to come up with what they did.

In my quest to share my love and appreciation of Chinese food, I myself have been blamed for 'dumbing down' Chinese cuisine for the Western palate in my attempt to whet people's appetite for it. But I much prefer to see it as 'creative fusion'. If I remained true to the Chinese classics, I would be a copycat cook and not a progressive one. A cook's job in my opinion is to be creative and push the boundaries of their cuisine and never stop experimenting.

Yes, classics are good, but classics at one point in history came from somewhere too. They were once new – someone invented them, and if they had never experimented, we wouldn't be enjoying those dishes today.

And are classic dishes the only authentic ones? I prefer the term 'heritage'. Dishes can have heritage and influence, but they are not necessarily 'authentic' because the

question would be, authentic to whom? Authenticity is a matter of perspective. Chinese takeaways have become such a staple of so many different countries that you could argue that they are just as authentic within immigrant Chinese cooking as the older, classic dishes.

I am always being asked for takeaway menu recipes, so here is my book on the subject. Don't accuse me of not knowing my *xiao long bao* from my *char siu bao* – because I do and I can make both. I want to share my love of Chinese takeaways and show how, cooked well, they can hold their own with the other great cuisines of the world. People also ask me whether I cook other types of food at home, and I certainly do. In fact, I have a soft spot for Lebanese cuisine, and I love Italian and Indian. But my vocation and career is making Chinese food – and please excuse the generic word 'Chinese', for there are over 34 regions in China with over 54 different dialects and each region has a unique way of preparing food. So until I master all the Chinese dishes there are to be mastered and explored, I won't be able to venture properly into other cuisines. Chinese cooking alone could keep me going for more than a lifetime.

If you are Chinese and, like my father, snobbish about Chinese takeaways, my hope is that, after reading these recipes, you will be cooking and feeding them to your kids instead of the dog and you will feel encouraged to embrace them as part of your culture and be proud of them.

Chinese takeaway cuisine is perfectly acceptable at home too, and I want to prove that, when cooked correctly, it can be the healthiest, most economical and delicious food you have ever eaten. With many low-fat dishes and using plenty of fresh vegetables and lean meat and fish, it's also good for those who are worried about keeping slim. If you are vegetarian, Chinese food has a huge array of bean curd and 'mock meat' recipes made from wheat gluten. Equally, if you are allergic to wheat or gluten or to monosodium glutamate, you can buy soy sauces that are wheat-free and condiments that don't contain MSG. If you have a nut allergy, use vegetable or sunflower oil instead of groundnut oil, and if you are watching your salt intake you can substitute a low sodium, light soy sauce. I would also advise using organic or free-range eggs and meat wherever possible.

With this book, I want to give you my 21st-century version of the Chinese takeaway, inspired by this favourite fast food. I want to demonstrate how I think Chinese takeaway dishes should be cooked at home. I will look at all the offerings, whether healthy or unhealthy, give my view on them, share tips with you and show you lots of easy recipes that can be cooked far more quickly than it would take you to order your favourite takeaway dish. I will share with you my knowledge of flavour pairings to get the best out of your Chinese store cupboard (see the box above for my top ten ingredients) and introduce some new ways of eating and cooking Chinese food. In addition, I want to show you how Chinese takeaway dishes, when cooked with the freshest ingredients you can lay your hands on (coupled with the right culinary techniques), is a far superior 'fast food' than any other cuisine in the world. If I owned a takeaway, the dishes in this book are the ones you'd find on my menu.

Enough said. Less talk and more cooking!

MY TOP TEN ESSENTIAL CHINESE STORE-CUPBOARD INGREDIENTS:

1. Light soy sauce

2. Dark soy sauce

3. Shaohsing rice wine

4. Toasted sesame oil

5. Five-spice powder

6. Sichuan peppercorns

7. Chinkiang black rice vinegar

8. Clear rice vinegar

9. Chilli bean sauce

10. Chilli sauce

Ching 薺 x

Breakfast

When I first arrived in South Africa, I was five and a half. After a tearful goodbye to the rest of the family, my mother, brother and I packed our bags to join my father, who had already left to set up a bicycle business in South Africa. In Taiwan he had been working as a manager in a building company and hated his job. So when by chance he met Robert ('Uncle Robert' to us) and the South African convinced my father to set up in business with him, he jumped at the idea. We liked Uncle Robert: we had met him only once, but he had taken us to a pizza restaurant and given me a cuddly racoon toy from South Africa. Despite no previous business experience and not knowing a word of English, my father moved us all over there on a whim. It was to be one of the scariest but most fulfilling adventures of my childhood.

At Uncle Robert's insistence, we stayed on his farm just outside Jo'burg. He and his wife Susan accommodated us in a converted barn on their plot of land, which extended for acres and acres. They even had a mini reservoir with their own supply of water and they kept horses and several Rhodesian Ridgebacks. Aunty Susan was a welcoming lady. The day we arrived, while my mother was unpacking and tidying up the barn, she took us food shopping. My brother and I were taken to the most enormous building we had ever seen. It was a hypermarket. Back in Taiwan, I hadn't even been to a supermarket before. Even in Taipei, the only modern outlets we had were 7-Eleven convenience stores. The only place like it in our experience was the local wet market my grandmother used to take us to in the village, so this vast building was a shock.

My brother and I went up and down the aisles, admiring the rows and rows of packaged ingredients. There were even fish tanks with fresh lobsters and crabs. Aunty Susan guided us to a large chilled section; I remember feeling really cold. She pointed to the shelves and gestured to us to pick something, so I picked a small light brown carton and my brother picked a dark brown one. We hadn't a clue what we had chosen. The rest of that shopping trip is now hazy, although I remember plenty of boxes and paper bags being carted to Aunty Susan's large fancy kitchen.

She handed us each a teaspoon and we left her to her unpacking. I opened the foil lid of my carton and took a small mouthful, and my brother did the same. The taste was creamy and sour but also sweet; I had no idea that I had picked a caramel-flavoured yoghurt and my brother a chocolate one. We were used to our Yakult, but this was an entirely new experience. We weren't sure we liked it, but we went back to the barn and showed the yoghurts to Mum. She took a small mouthful and then spat it out: 'Pai kee yah!' ('It's gone off!' in Taiwanese). She stormed over to Aunty Susan's and started 'communicating' with her. They couldn't understand what each other were saying; in

the end my mum threw the pots in the bin! Aunty Susan looked bewildered and shrugged her shoulders. I thought Mum was rude, but I didn't dare say anything. The next day Aunty Susan dropped by as Mum was making us fried eggs for breakfast. She brought over these dark green, what my mum called *hulu-* or gourd-shaped vegetables. Aunty Susan sliced one in half to reveal a large round stone in the middle; she then scooped the green flesh out of one of the halves and smeared it on to a slice of brown bread she had brought over with her. She gestured to my mother to take a bite. My mum had a taste and shook her head, saying, 'Bu hao chi' ('Not good eat'). 'Avocaaaa-do,' said Aunty Susan, then smiled, patted us on our heads and walked out the door.

Despite not liking the taste, my mother hated wasting food, so she placed the eggs she had been frying on the avocado bread, drizzled over some soy sauce and told us to eat it. She didn't have any herself. Over time, however, avocados became one of my Mum's favourite foods. She now lives permanently in Taiwan, where avocados are hard to get and expensive. When we Skype, she will often ask, 'You still eating avocados?' That recipe, washed down with a glass of soya milk, is now one of my favourite dishes for breakfast.

You will notice that my recipes, like yin and yang, tend to be very black and white, very Western or very Chinese, but when recipes work together, East and West can be balanced, like the takeaway menu, to give amazing, what I like to call 'fu-sian'-style food. You may not associate breakfast with Chinese takeaways, but there are many eateries all over Asia that serve warming breakfasts, which can be bought on the way to school or work. In addition to Western-style sandwiches, these small eateries (and sometimes street stalls) serve *you-tiao*, or fried bread sticks, with hot or cold soya milk (sweetened or unsweetened), mantou (steamed buns) with savoury or sweet fillings and of course steaming bowls of congee in a variety of flavours. If I had a takeaway or diner, I would definitely include a breakfast menu, and I would serve a variety of Western and Chinese-style treats – just like the snack stalls in the East.

Toast with avocado, fried eggs and soy sauce

Aunty Susan, whom we stayed with when we first arrived in South Africa, gave my mother two ripe avocados, smearing one of them on some bread. Mum thought it was odd to serve a vegetable in this way, but soon she started to make us fried-egg sandwiches for breakfast with a generous slathering of avocado. Now I don't hesitate to make this for breakfast, spreading slices of toast with a chunky rich layer of ripe avocado, topped with poached or fried eggs (preferably sunny side up) and a drizzle of light soy sauce. If I had my own takeaway or diner, this would certainly feature on the menu!

PREP TIME: 5 minutes • **COOK IN:** 3 minutes • **SERVES:** 1

1 tbsp of groundnut oil

2 large eggs

2 slices of seeded rye bread

½ ripe avocado (save the rest for a salad later), stone removed and flesh scooped out

Drizzle of light soy sauce

Salt and ground black pepper

1. Heat a wok over a medium heat until it starts to smoke and then add the groundnut oil. Crack the eggs into the wok and cook for 2 minutes or to your liking. (I like mine crispy underneath and still a bit runny on top.) Meanwhile, place the bread in the toaster and toast for 1 minute.

2. To serve, place the toast on a plate and spread with the avocado flesh. Place the eggs on top and drizzle over the soy sauce, then season with salt and ground black pepper and eat immediately. This is delicious served with a glass of cold soya milk, a cup of rooibos tea with a slice of lemon or some freshly pressed apple or orange juice.

Basil omelette with spicy sweet chilli sauce

In Taiwan, there are many night market stalls that sell the famous oyster omelette. A little cornflour paste is stirred into beaten eggs, then small oysters are added and sometimes herbs. When the eggs have almost set, a spicy sweet chilli sauce is drizzled over the top, making a comforting, moreish snack. I adore this dish, but it is hard to get fresh small oysters, so I make a vegetarian version sometimes for breakfast, using sweet basil, free-range eggs and adding my own spicy sweet chilli sauce, made using condiments from my Chinese store cupboard.

PREP TIME: 3 minutes • **COOK IN:** 5 minutes • **SERVES:** 1

3 eggs
Large handful of Thai or
   Italian sweet basil leaves
Pinch of salt
Pinch of ground white pepper
1 tbsp of groundnut oil
Handful of mixed salad leaves,
   to garnish

FOR THE SAUCE

1 tbsp of light soy sauce
1 tsp of vegetarian oyster
   sauce
1 tbsp of mirin
1 tsp of tomato ketchup
1 tsp of Guilin chilli sauce,
   or other good chilli sauce

1. Make the spicy sweet chilli sauce by whisking all the ingredients together in a bowl, then set aside.

2. Crack the eggs into a bowl, beat lightly and add the basil leaves, then season with the salt and ground white pepper.

3. Heat a wok over a high heat until it starts to smoke and then add the groundnut oil. Pour in the egg and herb mixture, swirling the egg around the pan. Let the egg settle and then, using a wooden spatula, loosen the base of the omelette so that it doesn't stick to the wok. Keep swirling any runny egg around the side of the wok so that it cooks. Flip the omelette over if you can without breaking it, then fold and transfer to a serving plate, drizzle over some of the spicy sweet chilli sauce and serve with a garnish of mixed leaves.

Smoked salmon and egg fried rice

This is my classic breakfast recipe – it's so good I had to share it with you. Make sure you add the smoked salmon after the rice, as the rice acts as a cushion, helping the salmon not to catch on the side of the wok and flake into tiny pieces.

PREP TIME: 5 minutes • **COOK IN:** 7 minutes • **SERVES:** 1

1½ tbsps of groundnut oil

2 eggs, beaten

75g (3oz) frozen peas

300g (11oz) cooked leftover cold jasmine rice (see the first tip on page 186) or freshly cooked long-grain rice (see the tip below)

150g (5oz) smoked salmon, sliced into strips

1–2 tbsps of light soy sauce

1 tbsp of toasted sesame oil

Pinch of ground white pepper

1. Heat a wok over a high heat until it starts to smoke and then add 1 tbsp of the groundnut oil. Tip the beaten eggs into the wok and stir for 2 minutes or until they are scrambled, then remove from the wok and set aside.

2. Return the wok to a high heat and add the remaining groundnut oil, allowing it to heat for 20 seconds. Tip in the frozen peas and stir-fry for just under a minute. Add the cooked rice and mix well until the rice has broken down.

3. Add the smoked salmon slices and toss together for 1 minute, then add the scrambled egg pieces back into the wok and stir in. Season with the soy sauce (to taste), the toasted sesame oil and white pepper and serve immediately.

> **CHING'S TIP**
> If using freshly cooked rice, use 150g (5oz) of uncooked long-grain rice, such as basmati, rinse it well and then boil in 300ml (½ pint) of water, cooking until all the water has been absorbed. This will take an extra 20 minutes.
>
> **ALSO TRY**
> If you are not a fan of fish, then used smoked bacon lardons instead – cook them until crispy before adding.

Cumberland sausage, green pepper and tomato fried rice with pineapple

A few years ago, I came up with bacon and egg fried rice, which my friends adored. This one is a follow-on from that. It's the ultimate brunch dish – so easy to do on a lazy Sunday. Children will love it and the neighbours will hate you as they spy enviously over the fence while you tuck in. This is my equivalent of a fry-up, but avoid using too much oil in this dish, as the sausages are quite fatty. It's best to pour the excess fat away, as revealed below. For a healthier version of this dish, you could mix in some spinach leaves, if you liked, and serve with a simple garden salad.

PREP TIME: 10 minutes • **COOK IN:** 7 minutes • **SERVES:** 4

2 cloves of garlic, finely chopped

2.5cm (1in) piece of root ginger, peeled and finely sliced into matchsticks

6 Cumberland sausages (350g/12oz in total), chopped into 1.5cm (⅝in) rounds

1 green pepper, deseeded and cut into 1.5cm (⅝in) dice

1 very large ripe beef tomato, cut into chunks

500g (1lb 2oz) cold leftover cooked jasmine rice (see the first tip on page 186) or freshly cooked long-grain rice (see the tip below)

1 tbsp of light soy sauce

1 tbsp of chilli oil

Juice of 1 lemon

Large handful of ripe pineapple chunks

1. Heat a wok over a high heat until it starts to smoke. Add the garlic and ginger and stir-fry for a few seconds, then add the sausages and cook on a medium heat for 3–4 minutes, stirring constantly. Remove from the heat and pour away the excess oil.

2. Return the wok to the heat, add the pepper and stir-fry for 1–2 minutes, then add the tomato and toss all the ingredients together. Add the cooked rice, breaking it up well, especially if it has been in the fridge overnight.

3. Season with the soy sauce, chilli oil and lemon juice, then mix in the pineapple chunks, remove from the heat and serve immediately. Delicious with a glass of cold lemonade.

> **CHING'S TIP**
> If using freshly cooked rice, use 250g (9oz) of uncooked long-grain rice, such as basmati, rinse it well and then boil in 500ml (18fl oz) of water, cooking until all the water has been absorbed. This will take an extra 20 minutes.

Pork, ginger and duck egg congee

This is one of my favourite breakfast dishes. The famous *cha chaan teng* tea restaurants in Hong Kong serve it, especially the ones located in the old wet market at Canton Road in Kowloon. I love visiting the wet markets there; I usually go shopping early for ingredients and then reward myself with a steaming bowl of this congee.

PREP TIME: 10 minutes • **COOK IN:** 65 minutes • **SERVES:** 4–6

2 century eggs, each sliced into quarters and halved lengthways

1 tbsp of groundnut oil

2.5cm (1in) piece of root ginger, peeled and finely sliced

200g (7oz) pork fillet, finely sliced

1 tbsp of Shaohsing rice wine, dry sherry or vegetable stock

3 shiitake mushrooms, finely diced

2 tbsps of light soy sauce

Salt and ground white pepper

Dash of toasted sesame oil (optional)

2 spring onions, finely sliced, to garnish

FOR THE CONGEE

250g (9oz) jasmine rice or 200g (7oz) jasmine rice and 50g (2oz) glutinous rice

250ml (9fl oz) vegetable stock

1. First make the congee. Pour the rice into a large heavy-based saucepan, add the stock and 700ml (1¼ pints) of water and bring to the boil. Once boiled, reduce the heat to medium-low, place a tight-fitting lid on the pan and allow to simmer, stirring occasionally to make sure the rice does not stick to the side and bottom of the pan.

2. After the rice has been cooking for 45 minutes, add the duck egg pieces and continue to cook for a further 20 minutes.

3. Meanwhile, heat a wok over a high heat until it starts to smoke. Add the groundnut oil and ginger slices and stir-fry for a few seconds, then add the pork slices and stir for 1 minute or until they start to turn brown. Add the rice wine (or sherry or vegetable stock) and cook for a further minute, then tip in the mushrooms and season with the soy sauce.

4. Add the pork stir-fry to the cooked congee and stir in well. Season, add a dash of sesame oil, if you like, and sprinkle over the sliced spring onions. Serve immediately with chunks of *you-tiao* (fried bread sticks), if you have any, for a truly traditional Chinese breakfast.

Big bowl of oat congee and accompaniments – 'The Works'

This is not for the faint-hearted – like eating 'smelly porridge', as my other half describes it. But if you are a fan of durian, stinky dofu and century eggs, then you will love the complex flavours of this dish. The fermented bean curd blends in with the sweetness of the seaweed paste and picks up the fiery pungency of the pickled bamboo shoots, while the pickled lettuce delivers a refreshingly vinegary sweetness that cuts through the richness of all the other ingredients.

This dish brings back memories and instantly I am transported to my grandmother's farm, where daily breakfast treats would be a rotation of these ingredients, along with a small bowl of hot steaming congee (or rice porridge). Rice porridge takes too long for me to make in the morning, so I now have oat porridge instead. When I prepare this, assembling all the ingredients, it is like a meditation process and nostalgia trip rolled into one. Nothing can get in the way and I feel depressed when I run out of any of the components. You may be surprised and perhaps even disgusted by this strange obsession of mine, but I invite you to try the dish with courage and an open mind.

PREP TIME: 5 minutes • **COOK IN:** 6 minutes • **SERVES:** 1

100g (3½oz) rolled oats

1 tbsp of groundnut oil

2 eggs

5–6 chives or 1 spring onion, finely chopped (optional)

1 tbsp of light soy sauce

FOR THE ACCOMPANIMENTS

4–5 pickled soy lettuce stems

1 tsp of momoya (Japanese seaweed paste)

1 tbsp of salted roasted peanuts

1 tbsp of pickled bamboo shoots in chilli oil

2 tbsps of dried pork floss

½ small cube of dofu (fermented bean curd)

1. Place the oats in a saucepan with 200ml (7fl oz) of water and bring to the boil, then reduce the heat and cook for 3–4 minutes, stirring frequently, or until the mixture has thickened.

2. Meanwhile, heat a small wok or frying pan over a medium heat until it starts to smoke and then add the groundnut oil. Crack in the eggs, sprinkle over the chopped chives or spring onion (if using) and fry the eggs to your liking.

3. Transfer to a plate and drizzle over the soy sauce. Pour the porridge into a bowl, arrange all your accompaniments on top (like the different colours on a painter's palette) and then mix and eat straight away with the eggs.

Soups

I adore Chinese soups – the classic takeaway offerings and the more exotic ones. The nourishing soups my grandmother used to make for me using Chinese herbs like cassia twigs, red dates, *Angelica sinensis*, rhizome of rehmannia and others that I cannot pronounce were a staple in my family kitchen. Both my mother and grandmother insisted that we have these herbal broths, often cooked with a little meat, such as *lao-ji* (old organic chicken) or *pai-gu* (pork ribs). This was based on the belief that these traditional Chinese herbs replenish the 'yang' *chi* (energy) thought to be good for a woman's 'system', keeping her fertile and youthful. My grandmother especially loved stewing these herbal concoctions and the meat she typically included would be pig's trotters or chicken's feet, believing that their gelatinous texture would help keep skin plump and beautiful – and I believe her, because grandmothers always know best. I never argued with my grandmother when it came to food; she was the food royalty in my family, the queen bee, and her opinion was always the final word on the subject.

I grew up not turning my nose up at such dishes because this was the norm in my family. I only realised that these treasured family recipes were 'different' when my school friend Lina came over for dinner one Saturday night. I had recently moved from South Africa to London and had just started secondary school. Lina, of Lebanese origin, was the bubbliest girl at school and one of the most popular, so I was excited that she was coming round. My mother went to a Chinese supermarket and brought back the

freshest ingredients. When asked what we were having for dinner, my mother pointed to a shiny red bucket with a bamboo steamer lid over it. We both took a peek and, to Lina's horror, were greeted by two fat river eels writhing about in the water and staring up at us. My mum was planning to cook her herbal eel soup for us. I will never forget the look on Lina's face! Needless to say, she didn't stay for dinner and didn't come round again for a very long time, let alone for dinner. When she eventually invited me to her house, I was greatly relieved that the 'eel experience' had not damaged our friendship.

Her family were so welcoming. It was a treat to watch her mother make houmous from scratch, her *tete* (grandmother) make the flatbread and tabouleh, and her father orchestrate the cooking of shish taouk and lamb shawarmas on their gigantic home-built barbecue. Everything smelt wonderful. We all sat around a large table and feasted together. Her father, a proud, eccentric man, made sure I had plenty to eat and my plate stayed full. I was enjoying everything until he winked at me to try a dish of what looked like very small sausages … so I did. The whole room exploded in laughter; her brother patted me on my back and declared, 'How were the sheep's testicles, Ching?!' Wide-eyed, I turned to look at him and nearly spat the piece of 'sausage' in his face. So Lina and I were quits, and neither episode was ever mentioned again.

Lina and I continued to have many more culinary adventures together as our friendship developed. I once tried making her and some other schoolfriends chicken and sweetcorn soup, which was far too watery because it was the first large-batch cooking I had ever attempted. When we reached sixth form, sometimes we had no classes after lunch, so we would hitch the 240 bus from Mill Hill to Golders Green in search of satisfying our cravings for wonton soup or beef and black bean soup with ho fun noodles. Our destination was the Water Margin in Golders Green, where we would gossip about school or pour our hearts out over boys we fancied while sipping from a bowl of crabmeat and sweetcorn soup or hot and sour soup, dishes that comforted us and seemed to echo the sour-sweet times as teenagers living in London and trying to fit in. We fought to fit in at school, struggling with our cultural differences and desperate to find our identity, but food connected us.

My mother's herbal eel soup may have tested my friendship with Lina, but it will always remind me of who I am and where I come from. I believe the strongest relationships are built on such experiences. I once overheard my mother on the phone to her friend; they were talking about a lady within the Chinese community whose English husband was apparently filing for divorce because he had caught her eating fish-head soup! The lesson I learned was that if those close to you accept your food choices, no matter how weird, they are true friends. In case you want to test this out yourself, I have included Mum's Herbal Eel Soup (see page 37) for you to try.

One thing is for sure, when I'm feeling under the weather, when there are dramas going on or I'm plagued by worry, I always make a comforting bowl of soup and I get my perspective back again. I have included some of my takeaway favourites here and given some a makeover.

Tomato and egg flower soup

Classic egg flower or egg drop soup (*dan hua tang*) – 'egg flower' describing the web-like pattern made by the egg when dropped into the hot liquid – is easy to make and very nutritious. You can add other ingredients to this soup, such as cubes of fresh dofu, baby prawns or dried seaweed (nori), or, for a more substantial dish, cooked egg noodles for a quick, light supper.

PREP TIME: 5 minutes • **COOK IN:** 10 minutes • **SERVES:** 2

1 tbsp of vegetable bouillon powder or stock powder

3 ripe tomatoes, sliced (see the tip below)

2 eggs, lightly beaten

1 tbsp of light soy sauce

Dash of toasted sesame oil

Pinch of sea salt

Pinch of ground white pepper

1 tbsp of cornflour mixed with 2 tbsps of water

Large handful of baby spinach (optional)

2 spring onions, finely sliced, to garnish

1. Pour 500ml (18fl oz) of water into a large saucepan and bring to the boil. Add the bouillon or stock powder and stir to dissolve. Reduce the heat to a simmer, then add the tomatoes and cook on a medium heat for 5 minutes or until the tomatoes have softened.

2. Pour the beaten eggs into the broth, stirring gently. Add the soy sauce, toasted sesame oil, salt, pepper and cornflour paste and mix well until slightly thickened. Add the spinach (if using) and let it wilt, then garnish with the spring onions and serve immediately.

CHING'S TIP
I don't bother skinning tomatoes – most of the nutrients are just beneath the skin after all – but if you want to skin them before slicing first cut a small cross at the base of each tomato. Plunge them into a wok or saucepan of boiling water for less than 1 minute, then drain. The skin will peel off easily.

Traditional hot and sour soup

This is one of my all-time favourite soup recipes. It transforms store-cupboard staples into an amazing dish. There may seem to be a long list of ingredients, but the end result is worth it because they all help to create layers of flavour and texture in this wonderfully warming winter dish.

PREP TIME: 20 minutes • **COOK IN:** 20 minutes • **SERVES:** 4

1 tbsp of vegetable bouillon powder or stock powder

1 tbsp of peeled and grated root ginger

2 red chillies, deseeded and finely chopped

300g (11oz) cooked chicken breast, shredded

1 tsp of Shaohsing rice wine or dry sherry

2 tbsps of dark soy sauce

1 x 220g tin of bamboo shoots, drained

10g (⅓oz) dried Chinese wood ear mushrooms, soaked in hot water for 20 minutes, drained and finely sliced

100g (3½oz) fresh firm dofu, cut into 1 x 5cm (½ x 2in) strips

50g (2oz) Sichuan preserved vegetables, rinsed and sliced (optional)

2 tbsps of light soy sauce

3 tbsps of Chinkiang black rice vinegar or balsamic vinegar

1 tbsp of chilli oil

Few pinches of white pepper

1 egg, lightly beaten

1 tbsp of cornflour mixed with 2 tbsps of water

1 large spring onion, sliced

Handful of chopped coriander, to garnish (optional)

1. Pour 1 litre (1¾ pints) of water into a large saucepan and bring to the boil. Add the bouillon or stock powder and stir to dissolve. Bring back up to the boil and then add all the ingredients up to and including the wood ear mushrooms. Reduce the heat to medium, then add the dofu, Sichuan vegetables (if using), soy sauce, vinegar, chilli oil and white pepper and simmer for 10 minutes.

2. Stir in the egg, then add the cornflour paste and stir to thicken the soup (adding more cornflour paste if you like a thicker consistency). Add the spring onion, garnish with the coriander, if you like, and serve immediately.

CHING'S TIP
If you love your spicy heat, just increase the amount of chillies.

ALSO TRY
You can substitute the chicken with shiitake mushrooms for a vegetarian version of this dish.

Watercress soup with pork, mushroom and ginger wontons

Probably one of the most popular takeaway soups, this is also a personal favourite. I love these dumplings in a clear broth. The ones we used to have at the Water Margin were large and plump with a prawn and pork filling. This is my version; I like making mine small using small wonton egg wrappers, which you can easily pick up from a Chinese supermarket. The beauty of this dish is that you can serve it for a casual dinner or an elegant supper – versatile, like a pair of trusted black patent Fendi boots.

PREP TIME: 20 minutes • **COOK IN:** 10 minutes • **SERVES:** 4

28 wonton wrappers
(7.5cm/3in square)
1 egg, beaten
700ml (1¼ pints) vegetable
stock

FOR THE FILLING
250g (9oz) minced pork
1 large spring onion, finely
chopped
3 shiitake mushrooms, finely
diced
1 tbsp of peeled and grated
root ginger
1 tbsp of Shaohsing rice wine
or dry sherry
1 tbsp of cornflour
Pinch of sea salt
Pinch of ground white pepper

TO SERVE
1–2 tbsps of toasted sesame oil
Small handful of watercress
leaves
1 spring onion, finely sliced

1. Place all the ingredients for the filling in a large bowl and mix together well.

2. To prevent the wrappers from opening up once cooked, brush the inside of each one with some of the beaten egg. Take one wonton wrapper and place a small tsp of the filling in the centre. Gather up the sides of the wrapper and mould around the filling into a ball shape, twisting the top to secure it. Repeat with the remaining wrappers.

3. To make the soup, pour the stock into a large saucepan and bring to a simmer. Add the wonton dumplings and cook for 5 minutes or until they all rise to the surface – like floating clouds, as the Chinese might say.

4. Pour the soup and dumplings into serving bowls, allowing 7 dumplings per person. Add a dash of toasted sesame oil to each bowl, scatter over a few of the watercress leaves (letting them wilt in the bowl), finish with a sprinkling of sliced spring onions and serve immediately.

> **CHING'S TIP**
> If any filling is left over, make more dumplings and freeze. They can be cooked from frozen for an emergency supper.

Pork rib, turnip and carrot broth with coriander

This is one of my grandfather's favourite recipes. It is not standard takeaway fare, but there are many takeaway and eat-in restaurants in Taiwan that serve this kind of pork rib soup (*pai-gu tang*) to accompany salty main dishes. Eaten between mouthfuls of the main dish, it works as a palate cleanser. It is a light sweet broth, the daikon (white radish) adding a slight bittersweetness to complement the meatiness of the pork ribs. When I eat it, it always reminds me of my grandmother's home cooking. If I had my own takeaway, this soup would be on the menu, no question.

PREP TIME: 10 minutes • **COOK IN:** 25 minutes • **SERVES:** 4

250g (9oz) pork ribs, cut into 2.5cm (1in) pieces

2 tbsps of vegetable bouillon powder or stock powder

350g (12oz) daikon (white radish), sliced into 1cm (½in) rounds, each cut into 6 wedges

2 carrots, cut into 1cm (½in) rounds, each quartered into wedges

1 tbsp Shaohsing rice wine or dry sherry

Sea salt and ground white pepper

Handful of roughly chopped coriander

1. Prepare the pork ribs by blanching them in boiling water for 2 minutes and then drain well. Bring 1 litre (1¾ pints) of water to the boil in a large saucepan and add the bouillon or stock powder, stirring it to dissolve.

2. Add the pork ribs, daikon, carrots and rice wine or dry sherry. Bring back up to the boil, then reduce the heat to medium-low and simmer for 20 minutes or until the vegetables are tender. Season with salt and ground white pepper, add the chopped coriander and serve immediately.

Posh crab and crayfish tail sweetcorn soup

To me, a good takeaway would serve this soup. It may be relatively expensive, but it is so worth it. I usually have a few tins of crabmeat and sweetcorn in my store cupboard and this makes a delicious quick, light supper. If you are entertaining, you can jazz up this recipe by topping it with some cooked crayfish tails and serve with some toasted rye bread and butter. You could also substitute the tinned crabmeat with fresh crabmeat for a treat.

PREP TIME: 5 minutes • **COOK IN:** 15 minutes • **SERVES:** 4

2 x 170g tins of crabmeat in brine, drained

2 x 200g tins of sweetcorn, drained

1 large ripe tomato, sliced

2 eggs, beaten

3 tbsps of light soy sauce

1 tbsp of toasted sesame oil

Sea salt and ground white pepper

2 tbsps of cornflour mixed with 4 tbsps of water

1 large spring onion, finely sliced

180g (6½oz) cooked crayfish tails in brine, drained

1. Pour 1 litre (1¾ pints) of water into a large wok or saucepan and bring to the boil. Add the crabmeat, sweetcorn and tomato and bring back up to the boil, then reduce the heat and simmer for 5 minutes.

2. Add the beaten eggs and stir gently to create a web-like pattern in the soup as the eggs start to cook. Season with the soy sauce, sesame oil and salt and pepper, adding more to taste if necessary. Bring to the boil and then stir in the cornflour paste to thicken the soup. Reduce the heat, sprinkle in the spring onion and leave to simmer on a gentle heat until ready to serve.

3. Ladle the soup into serving bowls, top with a few crayfish tails (which will warm through in the heat of the soup) and serve immediately.

ALSO TRY
You could substitute the crabmeat with cooked sliced chicken breast or, for a vegetarian option, use diced marinated dofu or sliced shiitake mushrooms (or chestnut mushrooms if you are on a budget). If you want a creamier consistency, use tins of creamed sweetcorn instead.

Mum's herbal eel soup

I wanted to include this more unusual recipe even though it doesn't really have a connection to Chinese takeaways in the West. In Hong Kong, on the other hand, there are eateries that serve herbal soups such as this to take away. Don't be put off by the sound of this soup – it's actually quite delicious, although admittedly an acquired taste. You will either love or hate it – for me, it's love. It's also very good for you. If you can, add a few dried goji berries to the soup 15 minutes before the cooking time is up; it lends a mellow sweetness to the broth. These, together with the other herbs, can be bought from a Chinese supermarket.

PREP TIME: 5 minutes • **COOK IN:** 65 minutes • **SERVES:** 4

600g (1lb 5oz) fresh river eel, head and tail discarded and any fins removed (or ask your fishmonger to do this for you)

2 tbsps of Shaohsing rice wine or dry sherry

½ tsp of salt

1 tbsp of vegetable bouillon powder or stock powder

5g (¼oz) *Angelica sinensis* (Chinese angelica or dong quai)

5g (¼oz) rhizome of rehmannia

8g (⅓oz) *Ligusticum wallichii* (Sichuan lovage)

5g (¼oz) matrimony vine

5 dried red dates

2 x 5cm (2in) sticks of cassia

1 x 5cm (2in) stick of cinnamon

Small handful of dried goji berries (optional)

1. Slice the eel into 5cm (2in) pieces, keeping the bones intact, then rinse well. Place the pieces in a large saucepan of boiling water to blanch for 2 minutes and then drain and set aside.

2. Place the blanched eels back in the pan. Pour in 1.5 litres (2½ pints) of water and add all the remaining ingredients except the goji berries. Bring to the boil, then reduce the heat and simmer for 1 hour or until the eel is tender and delicious. If using the goji berries, add these for the final 15 minutes of cooking.

ALSO TRY
If you're not so keen on the idea of cooking eel, then simply substitute it with chicken or pork ribs.

Appetisers

'No, Peking duck is better.' This is what my father would insist whenever he saw crispy aromatic duck on the menu at a Chinese restaurant. On one occasion I felt I had to intervene; I could see the disappointed look on the Swiss husband of one of my father's guests. I told my father I had a craving for crispy duck and he called me a *wai guo ren* (foreigner) in front of his friends, at which everyone laughed, the Swiss man included. I couldn't believe it! For the first time, I had put myself in the firing line to satisfy someone else's craving for a particular dish. On the plus side, I now occupied the moral high ground. I had been selfless in the sacrifice of my dignity for the happiness of another and thought my Buddhist master would be proud of my spiritual development (even if I was still a self-confessed carnivore).

Since my 'enlightening' crispy duck experience, I was actually enlightened once again, years later, to find that crispy aromatic duck is basically Chinese in origin and not something just concocted for foreigners, bearing a resemblance to tea-smoked Sichuan duck, Cantonese roast duck and Peking duck. All four dishes use Chinese five spice, the difference being that crispy aromatic duck is deep-fried rather than oven-roasted. When I told my father this, he still maintained in his father-knows-best tone that 'crispy duck is no good anyway because they fry the duck on its last days of freshness'.

Crispy aromatic duck seems to be confined to the UK. The debate continues about who invented it. According to the previous generation of Chinese food lovers, the Richmond Rendezvous Group – a chain of restaurants that created the boom in Chinese cuisine in the mid-1960s – was responsible for this delicious recipe that is consistently voted as the No. 1 Chinese takeaway dish in Britain.

Peking duck is equally popular: Beijingers see it as the national dish of China, the crème de la crème of all dishes. Chefs are super-proud of the delicious smoky golden skin of the duck and tender, succulent flesh, achieved by first slathering the bird in a maltose glaze and airdrying for eight hours before filling with water and cooking it in a wood-fired oven so that the meat is steamed on the inside while the outside remains crisp. At a good restaurant, the waiter will meticulously carve the skin and meat in front of you and serve the skin with some fine sugar. This will be served with thin steamed pancakes made from wheat flour, sliced cucumber, spring onions and a good *tian mian jiang* (sweet flour sauce). You should also expect a good restaurant to ask you how you would like the rest of the duck cooked – either in a delicious herbal broth soup or in a stir-fry with lush greens (I usually go with the chef's recommendation). Both Peking duck and crispy duck are on my top list of favourite starters, so they are both included in this chapter, although my version of Peking duck is more like Cantonese roast duck

because it is easier to recreate in the home kitchen.

I now have a tendency to judge dinner hosts based on their diplomacy when it comes to ordering (even if they are paying) and I am careful to be as sensitive as possible, to the point where I might be accused of being too nice. But better to be that, in my opinion, than greedy and selfish with no manners. There is a real art to ordering and being a good host; it takes real skill or *gong-fu* (kung fu). The Chinese are known for their generosity when it comes to dining, but a fine line needs to be trodden there as well: order too much and you look like a show-off; too little and you are seen as a scrooge. I take advice from my Buddhist master and that is: always finish what is on the table. It is better not to waste good food – think of all the people who go hungry.

When it comes to dinner parties at your own home, one thing is for sure: the very first dishes should impress. First impressions count. Like a teaser trailer to a blockbuster film, it should give you a hint of what to expect but without giving the whole plot away. It should excite and thrill you, satisfying you up to a point while leaving you hungry for more.

I usually serve a combination of 'yang' dishes, 'yang' being my label for 'fried' because it doesn't sound so bad. Yes, we all know that fried food comes with an 'unhealthy' tag, but it is all a matter of what you choose to eat. If you served and ate only fried food, you would soon be in A&E. Like everything in life, food choices are about balance. 'Yang' is appropriate because, in food terms, it means 'hot' energy, i.e. food that creates more 'heat' within the body. The opposite of this is 'yin' or cooling energy. It is not good for the body to be too 'yang', as it puts stress on the body. So my 'yang' menu carries this health warning – do not serve all these fried dishes in one meal; they are meant to be served only as an accompaniment to a variety of balanced dishes.

I have included many of my favourite naughty 'yang' takeaway starters (see pages 42–60) such as Pork and Prawn Fried Wantons and Crispy Sweet Chilli Beef Pancakes, my take on crispy duck pancakes. If this is all too 'yang' for you, then fear not, as I have also included some 'leng' starters, i.e. 'cooling' dishes that are more balanced and not fried (see pages 61–73).

Vegetable spring rolls (chun juen)

Some may think this isn't a traditional Chinese dish – but it is, usually eaten at the Spring Festival or Chinese New Year. It has northern Chinese roots where wheat flour is the main form of carbohydrate and *bings* – semi-rolled pancakes – are eaten, with various delicious fillings wrapped inside.

PREP TIME: 20 minutes, plus 10 minutes for cooling
COOK IN: 7 minutes • **MAKES:** 12 small rolls

600ml (1 pint) groundnut oil

1 tsp of peeled and grated root ginger

100g (3½oz) shiitake mushrooms, sliced

100g (3½oz) tinned bamboo shoots, drained and cut into matchsticks

1½ tbsps of light soy sauce

1 tbsp of Chinese five-spice powder

75g (3oz) bean sprouts

2 large spring onions, sliced lengthways

1 small carrot, cut into matchsticks

1 tbsp of vegetarian oyster sauce

Pinch of sea salt

Pinch of ground white pepper

24 small spring roll wrappers (14.5cm/6in square)

1 tbsp of cornflour mixed with 1 tbsp of water

1. Heat a wok over a high heat until it starts to smoke and then add 1 tbsp of the groundnut oil. Add the ginger and stir-fry for a few seconds. Tip in the mushrooms and bamboo shoots and stir-fry for 1–2 minutes, then season with 1 tbsp of the soy sauce and the five-spice powder. Remove from the wok and set aside to cool for 10 minutes.

2. Put the bean sprouts, spring onions and carrot into a bowl, add the fried mushrooms and bamboo shoots and season with the oyster sauce, remaining soy sauce and the salt and pepper. Stir all the ingredients together to mix.

3. Take 2 spring roll wrappers and lay one on top of the other. (The extra layer will help prevent the skin from breaking.) Spoon 2 tbsps of filling into the centre of the top wrapper and brush each corner with the cornflour paste.

4. With the wrappers laid out in a diamond shape before you, bring the two side corners to meet in the middle, then bring the lower corner to the middle and roll the pastry with the filling towards the top corner. Tuck in the top edge and seal it with the cornflour paste. Continue in the same way until all the wrappers are filled.

5. Place a wok over a high heat and add the remaining groundnut oil. Heat the oil to 180°C (350°F) or until a cube of bread dropped in turns golden brown in 15 seconds and floats to the surface. Deep-fry the spring rolls for about 5 minutes or until golden brown, then remove with a slotted spoon and drain on kitchen paper. Serve with a dipping sauce, such as sweet chilli sauce, if you like.

CHING'S TIP
For a healthier 'baked' option, substitute the spring roll wrappers with 12.5cm (5in) squares of filo pastry. Brush one sheet with groundnut oil, cover with a second sheet and brush with oil again. Fill as in the recipe, then place on a baking tray and bake in the oven (preheated to 180°C/350°F/gas mark 4) for 20 minutes.

Crispy seaweed

This does not originate in China – it was invented by Chinese cooks in the West. It doesn't actually contain seaweed but is made with pak choy leaves that are finely shredded and deep-fried. I like to season mine with salt and granulated sugar so that it's sweet and salty. It's a great way to use up any pak choy you may have that is slightly past its best, and is also great as an appetiser or sprinkled as a garnish over crispy squid.

PREP TIME: 10 minutes • **COOK IN:** 2 minutes • **SERVES:** 2–4 to share

600ml (1 pint) groundnut oil

200g (7oz) pak choy leaves, stems removed

Sea salt and granulated sugar, for sprinkling

1 tsp of toasted white sesame seeds (see the tip below)

1. Place a wok over a high heat and pour in the groundnut oil. Heat the oil to 180°C (350°F) or until a cube of bread dropped in turns golden brown in 15 seconds and floats to the surface.

2. Add half the pak choy leaves and deep-fry for a few seconds, then lift out using a slotted spoon and drain on kitchen paper. Deep-fry the remaining pak choy leaves and drain in the same way.

3. Season the 'seaweed' with salt and sugar to taste, then transfer to a serving dish, sprinkle over the toasted sesame seeds and serve immediately.

> **CHING'S TIP**
> You can buy sesame seeds ready-toasted, but they taste much better if you toast them yourself. Simply add the raw seeds to a frying pan set over a medium heat and dry-fry, tossing occasionally, for 3–4 minutes or until they begin to brown and become fragrant. Keep a close eye on them, as they can quickly burn, and remove from the heat as soon as they are toasted.
>
> **ALSO TRY**
> For a non-vegetarian option, you could sprinkle over dried pork or fish floss instead of the toasted sesame seeds.

Sesame prawn toast

This dish is a takeaway classic. Instead of mincing the prawns, however, I keep them whole, wrapping them in brown toast and sesame seeds and then frying them until golden brown. They are delicious served with sweet chilli sauce.

PREP TIME: 15 minutes • **COOK IN:** 5 minutes • **MAKES:** 8 toasts

1 tsp of peeled and grated root ginger

1 large spring onion, finely chopped

1 egg, beaten

1 tbsp of cornflour

Dash of toasted sesame oil

Dash of light soy sauce

Salt and ground white pepper

8 tbsps of white sesame seeds, toasted (see the tip opposite)

4 slices of brown toast, halved and crusts removed

8 raw tiger prawns, shelled and deveined, tails left on

600ml (1 pint) groundnut oil

1. Combine the ginger, spring onion, beaten egg, cornflour, toasted sesame oil and soy sauce in a bowl and season with 2 pinches of salt and some white pepper. Place the sesame seeds in another bowl.

2. Dip a half piece of toast in the mixture and coat well. Then wrap the toast around a prawn and squeeze slightly so that the bread fully covers the prawn. Roll the wrapped prawn in sesame seeds and coat well. Repeat with the remaining prawns and pieces of toast.

3. Place a wok over a high heat, add the groundnut oil and heat to 180°C (350°F) or until a cube of bread dropped in turns golden brown in 15 seconds and floats to the surface. Deep-fry the sesame prawn toasts for 4–5 minutes or until golden brown, then remove with a slotted spoon, drain on kitchen paper and serve immediately.

'Stinky'-style aromatic dofu with kimchi

Stinky dofu is made by fermenting dofu in a pungent brine, which gives it a distinctive smell and flavour. Traditionally, the brine consists of fermented milk, dried prawns, mustard greens, bamboo shoots and Chinese herbs. It does smell strong, but it is extremely flavoursome. This dish is one of my favourite street-food snacks and I often have a craving for it. The dofu is deep-fried and served with sour cabbage and chilli sauce. This is my own version. I like to marinate dofu that has been already fried (and which you can buy in a Chinese supermarket) in garlic, mirin and five-spice powder, then deep-fry it and serve with some Korean-style kimchi and a good hot chilli sauce.

PREP TIME: 10 minutes, plus 1 hour for marinating
COOK IN: 3 minutes • **SERVES:** 2–4 to share

8 x 6cm (2½in) square pieces of deep-fried dofu
4 tbsps of potato flour or cornflour
600ml (1 pint) groundnut oil

FOR THE MARINADE
2 cloves of garlic, crushed and finely sliced
4 tbsps of mirin
1 tbsp of clear rice vinegar or cider vinegar
1 tsp of Chinese five-spice powder

TO GARNISH (OPTIONAL)
Pinch of medium chilli powder
Few sprigs of coriander

TO SERVE (IN SEPARATE DISHES)
3 tbsps of kimchi
2 tbsps of chilli bean sauce
2 tbsps of chilli sauce mixed with 2 tbsps of oyster sauce
2 tbsps of hot chilli sauce

1. Mix together all the ingredients for the marinade in a bowl and add the dofu pieces, then cover the bowl with cling film and leave to marinate for 1 hour. Lift the dofu pieces out of the marinade, giving them a good squeeze to remove any excess liquid, then dust with the potato flour or cornflour.

2. Place a wok over a high heat and add the groundnut oil. Heat the oil to 180°C (350°F) or until a piece of bread dropped in turns golden brown in 15 seconds and floats to the surface. Fry the dofu for 2–3 minutes or until golden and crisp on the outside, then drain on kitchen paper and cut into triangular wedges (each cut in half, diagonally, to give 16 triangles).

3. Transfer to a serving plate and dust with the chilli powder and sprinkle with the coriander if you like. Serve with the assortment of small dishes of kimchi, chilli bean sauce, chilli oyster sauce and hot chilli sauce.

Sichuan salt and pepper squid

Squid contains lots of nutrients, including zinc, manganese, copper, selenium and vitamin B12. When cooked well, it has a delicious soft, chewy texture. I was once fed squid sperm sacs stir-fried with egg and spring onions in a seafood restaurant in Hong Kong and it certainly was an acquired taste! Squid itself is not so challenging, however, and salt and pepper squid is one the most popular starters to be served in Chinese restaurants as well as appearing on some takeaway menus. This dish is easy to make and does not require much effort. I love the numbing heat from the Sichuan peppercorns: just dry-toast them in a pan and grind them well to ensure the maximum flavour.

PREP TIME: 15 minutes • **COOK IN:** 5 minutes • **SERVES:** 2–4 to share

1 egg, beaten

100g (3½oz) potato flour or cornflour

600ml (1 pint) groundnut oil

200g (7oz) squid, cleaned and sliced into rings

Salt

2 pinches of dried chilli flakes

1 tbsp of Sichuan peppercorns, toasted and ground (see the tip below)

Sprigs of coriander, to garnish

TO SERVE

Lemon wedges

Fruity Chilli Sauce (see page 57)

1. Mix the beaten egg with the potato flour or cornflour and 2 tbsps of water to make a batter.

2. Heat a large wok over a high heat and add the groundnut oil. Heat the oil to 180°C (350°F) or until a cube of bread dropped in turns golden brown in 15 seconds and floats to the surface.

3. Dip the squid rings into the batter and carefully drop into the hot oil. Deep-fry for 4–5 minutes or until golden, then lift out using a slotted spoon and drain on kitchen paper. Season with a little salt, the dried chilli flakes and ground toasted Sichuan peppercorns, then serve with lemon wedges and the Fruity Chilli Sauce and garnish with coriander sprigs.

CHING'S TIP
To toast the Sichuan peppercorns, heat a small wok or saucepan over a medium heat, then add the peppercorns and dry-toast for 1 minute or until fragrant. Transfer to a spice grinder or pestle and mortar and grind to a powder. Alternatively, place in a plastic bag and smash with a rolling pin.

Five-spice salted prawns with hot coriander sauce

This is my take on salt and pepper prawns: prawns coated in a starchy batter and deep-fried, then tossed in a spicy salt and served with a grapefruit and coriander dipping sauce. It also makes a sophisticated appetiser for serving with cocktails.

PREP TIME: 10 minutes • **COOK IN:** 5 minutes • **SERVES:** 2–4 to share

1 egg, beaten

100g (3½oz) potato flour or cornflour

600ml (1 pint) groundnut oil

12 raw tiger prawns, shelled and deveined, tails left on

FOR THE GRAPEFRUIT AND CORIANDER SAUCE

1 tbsp of peeled and grated root ginger

1 green chilli, sliced

1 red chilli, sliced

2 tbsps of lemon juice

Juice of ½ large pink grapefruit ('bits' included)

Handful of coriander leaves, finely chopped

FOR THE SPICE MIX

1 tsp of Chinese five-spice powder

1 tsp of sea salt

1 tsp of ground white pepper

1. Mix together all the ingredients for the sauce in a bowl and set aside. In a separate bowl, mix together the egg, potato flour or cornflour and 2 tbsps of water to make a batter. Set to one side.

2. Place a wok over a high heat, add the groundnut oil and heat to 180°C (350°F) or until a cube of bread dropped in turns golden brown in 15 seconds and floats to the surface.

3. Dip each prawn in the batter and then lower into the oil, one at a time. Cook for 4–5 minutes or until the prawns turn golden and then remove from the oil with a slotted spoon and drain on kitchen paper. Mix together the ingredients for the spice mix and sprinkle over the cooked prawns, toss well and eat immediately, served with the coriander sauce.

Japanese-style crispy halibut with lemon sauce

If you enjoy ordering lemon chicken from your local takeaway, then you will like this dish. It rather resembles English-style fish fingers – without the lemon sauce, that is! I like to use a good white-fleshed fish; cod is overfished, hence I've used halibut here, but pollack would do just as well. You could even use mackerel if you wished. I like using the Japanese panko breadcrumbs because they have been flavoured with honey and are extra crisp, but you could make your own breadcrumbs, of course, using a chunk of stale bread. The dipping sauce is easy to make too.

PREP TIME: 15 minutes • **COOK IN:** 5 minutes • **SERVES:** 2–4 to share

200g (7oz) halibut fillet, cut into 1cm (½in) strips

Sea salt and ground white pepper

100g (3½oz) potato flour or cornflour

1 egg, beaten

150g (5oz) panko breadcrumbs

600ml (1 pint) groundnut oil

Dried chilli flakes (optional)

Lemon wedges, to garnish (optional)

FOR THE SAUCE

1 tbsp of peeled and grated root ginger

1 tbsp of light soy sauce

1 tbsp of runny honey

1 tbsp of Shaohsing rice wine or dry sherry

100ml (3½fl oz) cold vegetable stock

50ml (2fl oz) lemon juice

1 tbsp of cornflour

1. Season the halibut pieces with salt and white pepper. Put the potato flour or cornflour, beaten egg and breadcrumbs in three separate bowls. Dip the halibut pieces into the potato flour or cornflour, then the egg and coat in the breadcrumbs.

2. Place a wok over a high heat and add all but 1 tbsp of the groundnut oil. Heat the oil to 180°C (350°F) or until a piece of bread dropped in turns golden brown in 15 seconds and floats to the surface. Fry the breaded halibut pieces in the oil for 3–4 minutes or until golden brown, then remove with a slotted spoon and drain on kitchen paper.

3. Meanwhile, make the sauce. Heat a small wok or saucepan over a medium heat and add the remaining 1 tbsp of groundnut oil. Add the ginger and fry for a few seconds, then add the remaining ingredients and bring to the boil. Cook for 1 minute or until the sauce has thickened, then remove from the heat.

4. When the fish is cooked, season with dried chilli flakes (if using), garnish with lemon wedges, if you like, and serve with the lemon dipping sauce.

Chinese-style soft-shell crabs

In Chinese cooking, crabs are served in a variety of ways, from steamed and braised as well as deep-fried. This is a popular dish, served in Chinese restaurants all over the world. It's also one of my favourite dishes.

Soft-shell crabs can be bought in the frozen sections of a Chinese supermarket. The most well-known variety is the blue crab from America. As the crabs grow, they moult their old shells and for a short period between May and July their new shell remains soft and delicate.

PREP TIME: 15 minutes, plus 20 minutes for marinating
COOK IN: 4 minutes • **SERVES:** 2–4 to share

4 frozen small soft-shell crabs, defrosted

2 eggs, beaten

200g (7oz) potato flour or cornflour

600ml (1 pint) groundnut oil

2 large pinches of sea salt

2 large pinches of ground black pepper

1 tsp of dried chilli flakes

FOR THE MARINADE

1 tbsp of groundnut oil

1 tbsp of peeled and grated root ginger

1 tsp of Shaohsing rice wine or dry sherry

1 tsp of Chinese five-spice powder

¼ tsp of medium chilli powder

1 tbsp of clear rice vinegar or cider vinegar

TO GARNISH

2 spring onions, finely sliced

2 red chillies, deseeded (optional) and sliced

1. To prepare a crab, first cut away the face (this can taste bitter), slicing behind the eyes. Next, lift the flap on the underside of the crab and cut this off. Loosen the top 'shell' of the body and lift it up to reveal the gills (plume-like filaments also known as 'dead man's fingers' – there are eight on each side of the crab's body). These are inedible and should be removed, along with any brown meat. Rinse the crab well and prepare the remaining crabs in the same way.

2. Mix together all the marinade ingredients in a bowl, then add the crabs, cover with cling film and leave to marinate for 20 minutes. In a separate bowl, mix together the eggs, potato flour or cornflour and 2 tbsps of water to make a batter.

3. Place a wok over a high heat and add the groundnut oil. Heat the oil to 180°C (350°F) or until a cube of bread dropped in turns golden brown in 15 seconds and floats to the surface.

4. Remove the crabs from the marinade and drain. Dip the crabs in the batter and then gently lower into the hot oil using a slotted spoon. Deep-fry for 3–4 minutes or until golden and then remove and drain on kitchen paper. Season with the salt, pepper and chilli flakes, then garnish with the spring onions and red chillies and serve immediately.

Sweet and sour Wuxi ribs

This dish originates from Wuxi in Zhejiang province. As this borders the neighbouring Shanghai municipality, it means that the dish can be found in many Shanghai restaurants too. The traditional way of preparing the ribs is to braise them slowly in stock for an hour, then add the sauce.

PREP TIME: 15 minutes, plus 20 minutes for marinating
COOK IN: 10 minutes • **SERVES:** 2–4 to share

600g (1lb 5oz) pork ribs, chopped into 3–4cm (1¼–1½ inch) pieces
400ml (14fl oz) groundnut oil
Sea salt and ground white pepper
1 spring onion, finely sliced, to garnish

FOR THE MARINADE
2 cloves of garlic, finely chopped
2 tbsps of yellow bean sauce
1 tbsp of Shaohsing rice wine or dry sherry

FOR THE SWEET AND SOUR SAUCE
2 tbsps of light soy sauce
2 tbsps of Chinkiang black rice vinegar or balsamic vinegar
1 tbsp of soft light brown sugar
1 tbsp of runny honey

1. Put all the ingredients for the marinade into a large bowl and stir to combine. Add the pork ribs and turn to coat, then cover the bowl with cling film and leave to marinate for at least 20 minutes in the fridge.

2. Place a wok over a high heat and add the groundnut oil. Heat the oil to 180°C (350°F) or until a cube of bread dropped in turns golden brown in 15 seconds and floats to the surface. Using a slotted spoon, carefully add the ribs and shallow-fry for 4–5 minutes or until browned and cooked through. Lift the ribs out of the wok and drain on kitchen paper.

3. While the ribs are cooking, place all the ingredients for the sweet and sour sauce in a small bowl and stir to combine.

4. Drain the wok of oil and wipe it clean, then place back over a high heat. Add the ribs and sauce mixture to the wok and cook on a medium-to-low heat for 5–6 minutes or until the sauce has reduced to a sticky consistency. Season to taste with salt and pepper, garnish with the spring onion and serve immediately.

Crispy sweet chilli beef pancakes

This is just like crispy duck pancakes but using beef instead of duck. The beef is coated in batter and then fried until crispy. To make a quick and easy sweet sauce, I have used a mixture of light soy, orange juice and shop-bought sweet chilli sauce.

PREP TIME: 20 minutes • **COOK IN:** 10 minutes • **SERVES:** 2–4 to share

300g (11oz) beef sirloin, fat removed, very finely sliced
2 tbsps of cornflour
600ml (1 pint) groundnut oil

FOR THE FRUITY CHILLI SAUCE
2 tbsps of light soy sauce
2 tbsps of sweet chilli sauce
Juice of 1 small orange

TO SERVE
2 carrots, cut into matchsticks
½ cucumber (unpeeled), cut into matchsticks
2 spring onions, finely sliced lengthways
12 small wheat-flour pancakes

ALSO TRY
If you like, you could turn this dish into crispy beef by adding fried beef pieces to the thickened sauce in the wok, tossing together and garnishing with orange zest.

1. Having prepared all the vegetables for serving, place them on a plate, cover with cling film and refrigerate.

2. Place the pancakes in a small bamboo steamer set over a saucepan of boiling water (making sure the bottom of the steamer doesn't touch the water) and steam for 5 minutes. Reduce the heat to low and keep the pancakes warm in the steamer until ready to serve.

3. Dip the beef strips in the cornflour, shaking off any excess flour, then place on a plate. Set a wok over a high heat and add the groundnut oil. Heat the oil to 180°C (350°F) or until a cube of bread dropped in turns golden brown in 15 seconds and floats to the surface. Deep-fry the beef for 4–5 minutes or until golden, then drain on kitchen paper.

4. While the beef is draining, place a small wok or frying pan over a high heat, add all the ingredients for the sauce and allow to bubble away until thickened.

5. Place the cooked beef on a serving plate and set on the table with the vegetables, warm sauce and pancakes, so that everyone can help themselves. To assemble a pancake, smear over some of the sauce, add a few strips of carrot, cucumber and spring onion, followed by a few pieces of crispy beef, then roll up and eat.

Pork and prawn fried wontons

These delicious wontons are deep-fried until golden and dipped in sweet and sour chilli sauce. This is a popular starter and you can vary the filling, using pork and Chinese mushrooms, pork and water chestnut or prawns and chives – the possibilities are endless.

PREP TIME: 20 minutes • **COOK IN:** 7 minutes • **SERVES:** 4

28 wonton wrappers (7.5cm/3in square)
1 egg, beaten
600ml (1 pint) groundnut oil

FOR THE FILLING
200g (7oz) minced pork
100g (3½oz) raw shelled and deveined freshwater shrimps or tiger prawns, roughly chopped
1 large spring onion, finely chopped
3 shiitake mushrooms, finely diced
1 tbsp of peeled and grated root ginger
1 tbsp of Shaohsing rice wine or dry sherry
1 tbsp of cornflour
Pinch of sea salt
Pinch of ground white pepper

1. Place all the ingredients for the filling in a bowl and mix well.

2. To prevent the wrappers from opening up and separating from the filling once cooked, brush the inside of each with the beaten egg. Take one wrapper and place a small tsp of the filling in the centre. Gather up the sides of the wrapper and mould around the filling into a ball shape, twisting the top to secure it. Repeat with the remaining wrappers, filling and moulding them in the same way.

3. Place a wok over a high heat and add the groundnut oil. Heat the oil to 180°C (350°F) or until a cube of bread dropped in turns golden brown in 15 seconds and floats to the surface. Deep-fry half the wontons for about 3 minutes or until golden, then remove with a slotted spoon and drain on kitchen paper. Repeat with the remaining wontons, then serve with the Fruity Chilli Sauce from page 57, if you like.

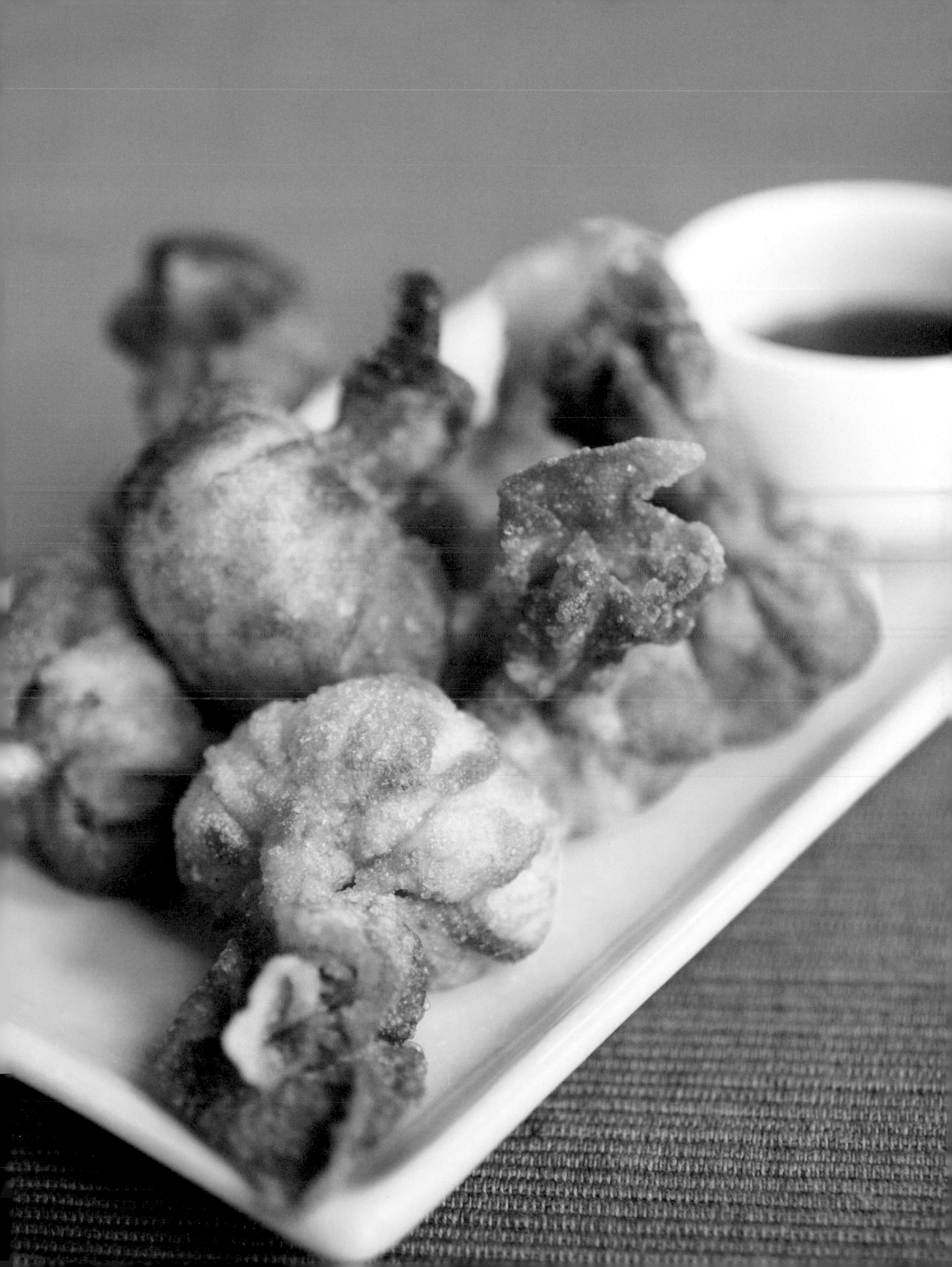

Fried sweet chilli chicken skewers

In the spirit of Westernised Chinese takeaway dishes, I have to admit this is my own contribution. It is naughty but very, very good – even if I say so myself.

PREP TIME: 15 minutes • **COOK IN:** 10 minutes • **SERVES:** 2–4 to share

3 large chicken thighs, skin on, deboned and halved

Sea salt and ground white pepper

4 tbsps of cornflour

2 egg whites

600ml (1 pint) groundnut oil

Small handful of chopped coriander

FOR THE SAUCE

3 cloves of garlic, finely chopped

2.5cm (1in) piece of root ginger, peeled and sliced

1 red chilli, deseeded and finely chopped

6 tbsps of sweet chilli sauce

1 tbsp of light soy sauce

Juice of 1 lime

SIX 8CM (3IN) BAMBOO SKEWERS (PRE-SOAKED IN WATER FOR 20 MINUTES TO PREVENT BURNING)

1. Thread each chicken piece on to a skewer, then season with salt and pepper. Place the cornflour and egg whites in a bowl and mix to make a batter.

2. Place a wok over a high heat and add the groundnut oil. Heat the oil to 180°C (350°F) or until a cube of bread dropped in turns golden brown in 15 seconds and floats to the surface.

3. Dip the chicken skewers in the batter, then lower into the oil and deep-fry for about 5 minutes or until crispy and golden. Lift out using tongs or a slotted spoon and drain on kitchen paper. Pour the oil from the wok through a sieve into a heatproof container.

4. To make the sauce, wipe out the wok and place back over a high heat. Add 1 tbsp of the drained oil, and when it starts to smoke, add the garlic, ginger and chilli and stir-fry for a few seconds, then add the remaining ingredients and mix well.

5. Return the cooked chicken to the wok and turn to coat in the hot sauce, then stir in the coriander and serve immediately.

Celery and dofu gan salad with sesame dressing

Dofu gan is dried firm bean curd or dofu that has virtually no moisture in it, unlike fresh bean curd. It is often stewed with soy sauce and lashings of Chinese five-spice and sugar. It is then drained, sliced and stir-fried, in true Sichuan fashion, with garlic, leeks, dried chillies and spring onions in a spiced chilli oil. I also like dofu gan sliced and served with *lu-dan* (hard-boiled eggs also stewed in the same mixture of soy sauce and spices). In some Chinese supermarkets you can buy ready-prepared dofu gan in vacuum packs, which you can then slice and make into this delicious chilled salad.

PREP TIME: 5 minutes, plus 30 minutes for chilling • **SERVES:** 2–4 to share

2 sticks of celery, cut on the diagonal into 5mm (¼in) slices

4 pieces of dofu gan (dried firm bean curd), sliced

Small handful of finely chopped coriander

FOR THE DRESSING

1 tsp of peeled and grated root ginger

½ tsp of chilli bean paste

1 tbsp of groundnut oil

1 tbsp of clear rice vinegar or cider vinegar

1 tbsp of mirin

1 tbsp of toasted sesame oil

1. Whisk together all the ingredients for the dressing in a bowl, add the celery and dofu gan pieces and turn in the dressing to coat. Cover with cling film and place in the fridge to chill for 30 minutes. Serve garnished with the chopped coriander.

Sesame green beans

Greens beans are delicious in any dish, whether eaten cold in salads or hot in stir-fries. They are at their very best in the middle of summer. When choosing green beans, go for ones that snap easily and have a smooth green, umblemished skin. They have a mild, fresh sweet flavour and are best cooked at a high temperature until crisp to lock in their colour and flavour. In China, they have a type of very long green bean known as a snake bean. These are usually deep-fried and then stir-fried so that they are tender and full of flavour. You can use snake beans in this recipe too, if you can get hold of them. This is a simple, quick recipe which can be served cold or hot, either as an appetiser or as an accompaniment to a main dish.

PREP TIME: 5 minutes, plus 30 minutes for chilling (if serving cold)
COOK IN: 2 minutes • **SERVES:** 2–4 to share

Salt

150g (5oz) French beans, topped and tailed, then chopped into 4cm (1½in) lengths

Black and white sesame seeds, toasted (see the tip on page 44), for sprinkling

FOR THE DRESSING

1 clove of garlic, crushed

2 tbsps of mirin

2 tbsps of light soy sauce

2 tbsps of clear rice vinegar or cider vinegar

2 tbsps of toasted sesame oil

1. Place the ingredients for the dressing in a bowl and mix well.

2. Bring a saucepan of salted water to the boil, add the beans and blanch for 2 minutes, then remove and drain.

3. If serving hot, transfer the beans to a bowl and toss in the dressing, then sprinkle over the toasted sesame seeds and serve immediately. If serving cold, rinse the warm beans in cold running water and drain well. Place in a dish, coat in the dressing and then cover with cling film and chill in the fridge for 30 minutes. Sprinkle over the toasted sesame seeds just before serving.

Victoria plums and heirloom tomatoes with sweet basil and salted plum shavings

This is a summer recipe at its best: great served as a starter to a Chinese-themed barbecue. Juicy heirloom tomatoes are delicious and full of flavour, although large ripe beef tomatoes would do instead. Couple these with Victoria plums and sweet basil leaves and you have my twist on the Italian caprese salad. What gives this dish extra punch is the sweet-sour shavings of Chinese preserved salted plum sprinkled over the top. If you have some Asian pears, you can peel them and add slices in between the tomatoes and plums to give a different texture.

PREP TIME: 10 minutes • **SERVES:** 4 to share

4 large ripe heirloom tomatoes or beef tomatoes, sliced

6 Victoria plums, peeled and stones removed, then sliced

2 Asian pears, peeled, cored and sliced (optional)

Handful of Thai or Italian sweet basil leaves

Pinch of sea salt

1 preserved salted plum, grated

FOR THE DRESSING

3 tbsps of extra-virgin olive oil

3 tbsps of aged balsamic vinegar

1. Arrange the tomatoes, Victorian plums, Asian pears (if using) and basil leaves in alternating layers on a serving plate.

2. Mix together the ingredients for the dressing and pour over the salad just before serving, sprinkling over the salt and the salted plum shavings to finish.

Pickled whole radishes with coriander

I am a big fan of radishes, of whatever kind. They come in a variety of shapes and colours, including the white Chinese radish or 'daikon'. Having lived in the West for most of my life, I have grown to love red radishes and look forward to them every spring and summer. My favourite are the French Breakfast radishes – long and elongated red and white roots like my two-tone Topshop Mary Jane shoes. This is one of my favourite pickled recipes – quick and easy and full of flavour, to get the tastebuds going.

PREP TIME: 5 minutes, plus 1 hour for marinating • **SERVES:** 2–4 to share

12 radishes (preferably French Breakfast), tops trimmed
Small handful of coriander, finely chopped, to garnish

FOR THE PICKLING LIQUID
3 tbsps of mirin
3 tbsps of clear rice vinegar or cider vinegar
1 tbsp of light soy sauce
½ tsp of caster sugar
Pinch of salt

1. Mix together all the ingredients for the pickling liquid in a shallow bowl. Drown the radishes in this, then cover with cling film, place in the fridge and leave to marinate for 1 hour. Serve sprinkled with the finely chopped coriander.

Cold sesame prawns and cucumber

For this dish, it really pays to use the sweetest cucumbers you can get your hands on: choose ones that are weighty and have a smooth, unwrinkled skin. I like using young tender small cucumbers if I can, as you don't need to deseed them and they add extra sweetness and crunch. This recipe makes the perfect summer appetiser, or it can be served as a lunch for two on a bed of watercress leaves and sliced yellow peppers. The dressing is quite delicious too.

PREP TIME: 5 minutes, plus 30 minutes for chilling • **SERVES:** 2–4 to share

150g (5oz) cooked shelled and deveined tiger prawns

½ cucumber (unpeeled), halved lengthways and cut into 5mm (¼in) slices

Black and white sesame seeds, toasted (see the tip on page 44), for sprinkling

5–6 chives, finely chopped, to garnish

FOR THE DRESSING

2 tbsps of mirin

2 tbsps of light soy sauce

2 tbsps of clear rice vinegar or cider vinegar

2 tbsps of toasted sesame oil

1. Place the prawns and cucumber slices in a serving bowl and mix together. Pour the ingredients for the dressing into another bowl and stir to combine, then add to the prawns and cucumbers and mix well. Cover with cling film, transfer to the fridge and chill for 30 minutes.

2. Just before serving, sprinkle over the toasted sesame seeds and garnish with the finely chopped chives.

Chilli crayfish tails and mango lettuce wraps

Some may think that crayfish tails are not a Chinese ingredient, but in fact China is the largest producer of crayfish in the world. Spicy Sichuan crayfish is a very popular restaurant dish, delicious washed down with a glass of cold beer. In the UK, supermarkets stock cooked crayfish tails preserved in brine. I love the flavour of crayfish tails; they are a real treat and make a change to prawns. This is one of my quick and easy 'fu-sian' starters, refreshing but with a hint of chilli, and great to make for a summer barbecue to serve with a variety of dishes.

PREP TIME: 10 minutes • **SERVES:** 2–4 to share

100g (3½oz) cooked crayfish tails in brine, drained

1 ripe mango, peeled and stone removed, then diced

8 sugar snap peas, sliced lengthways

Small handful of coriander, finely chopped, plus extra to garnish (optional)

1 red chilli, deseeded and finely chopped

Red Gem lettuce leaves, to serve

FOR THE SAUCE

3 tbsps of sweet chilli sauce

1 tbsp of fish sauce (nam pla)

1 tbsp of freshly squeezed lime juice

1 tbsp of freshly squeezed grapefruit juice

1 tbsp of extra-virgin olive oil

1. In a bowl, whisk together the ingredients for the sauce and set aside.

2. Add the crayfish tails to a serving dish and mix together with the mango, sugar snap peas, coriander (if using) and chilli.

3. Just before eating, spoon the sauce over the crayfish mixture and stir to combine. Garnish with a coriander sprig, if you like, and place on the table with a bowl of Red Gem lettuce leaves for people to help themselves. To assemble the dish, take a spoonful of the crayfish mixture, place in the middle of a lettuce leaf and eat immediately.

Cantonese-style roast duck and cucumber slices with salt and pepper

I am used to being served cold meats for a starter in a Chinese restaurant, such as beef shin in Sichuan spicy oil, cold roast Cantonese-style pork or cold chicken's feet. So I decided to make my own version of Cantonese-style roast duck, served cold with cucumber slices. A light, healthy dish, this can be easily pre-prepared for a dinner party and tastes delicious served with a glass of Riesling.

PREP TIME: 10 minutes, plus 30 minutes for cooling/chilling
COOK IN: 10 minutes • **SERVES:** 4 to share

2 x 250g (9oz) duck breasts, skin on

1 tbsp of Shaohsing rice wine or dry sherry

½ tsp of sea salt

2 tsps of Chinese five-spice powder

Sprig of coriander, to garnish (optional)

TO SERVE

1 cucumber (unpeeled), halved lengthways, deseeded and thinly sliced

2 spring onions, finely sliced

FOR THE SALT AND PEPPER MIX

1 tbsp of cracked sea salt

1 tbsp of ground white pepper

1. Preheat the oven to 220°C (425°F), gas mark 7.

2. Pierce the skin of the duck breasts with a fork, then pour over some boiling water and pat the skin dry with kitchen paper. The hot water helps to release some of the fat and ensure that the skin is crisp when cooked.

3. Place the duck breasts in a roasting tin, add the rice wine or dry sherry and season on both sides with the salt and Chinese five-spice powder. Roast for 10 minutes and then remove from the oven and leave to cool for a few minutes.

4. Once the duck has cooled down, cover with cling film and place in the fridge to chill for 20 minutes. To serve, slice and arrange on a serving plate, alternating with slices of cucumber and sprinkled with the finely sliced spring onions. Garnish with coriander sprigs, if you like. Mix together the cracked sea salt and white pepper in a small bowl and serve with the duck for dipping.

Cantonese-style roast duck with mango salad and plum dressing

This is a recipe I created when I was running my food kitchen in East London, although sadly it was never used because mangoes are quite expensive. It has now been resurrected and I proudly share it here. It makes a delectable starter, or for those watching their waistlines, it can also be served as a light supper.

PREP TIME: 10 minutes, plus 30 minutes for cooling/chilling
COOK IN: 10 minutes • **SERVES:** 2–4 to share

2 x 250g (9oz) duck breasts, skin on

1 tbsp of Shaohsing rice wine or dry sherry

½ tsp of sea salt

2 tsps of Chinese five-spice powder

FOR THE PLUM DRESSING

2 tbsps of plum sauce

2 tbsps of light soy sauce

2 tbsps of extra-virgin olive oil

4 tbsps of freshly squeezed orange juice

FOR THE SALAD

100g (3½oz) mixed salad leaves (such as watercress, baby spinach and rocket)

½ cucumber (unpeeled), halved lengthways and cut into 5mm (¼in) slices

2 spring onions, sliced lengthways

8 mangetout, finely sliced 3mm (⅛in) thick lengthways

1 ripe mango, peeled and stone removed, then sliced

1. For cooking and chilling the duck breasts, follow the instructions for Cantonese-style Roast Duck and Cucumber Slices with Salt and Pepper on page 68.

2. Meanwhile, whisk together all the ingredients for the plum dressing. Remove the duck from the fridge and cut into slices.

3. To assemble the dish, arrange the salad leaves, cucumber, spring onion and mangetout on a serving plate, place the sliced duck breast on top, then decorate with the mango slices, drizzle over a little of the dressing and serve.

ALSO TRY
If you like the texture of glass noodles, you could add pre-soaked ones to this dish and serve it as a refreshing noodle salad.

Mu shu pork

This dish originates from northern China. It traditionally consists of stir-fried pork and Chinese cabbage all finely chopped so that they can be served stuffed in steamed wheat-flour pancakes or buns. I have decided to vary the dish and, instead of the cabbage, use a tasty mixture of crunchy bamboo shoots, Chinese wood ear mushrooms and dry-roasted peanuts.

PREP TIME: 20 minutes • **COOK IN:** 10 minutes • **SERVES:** 4 to share

12 small wheat-flour pancakes

2 tbsps of groundnut oil

2 cloves of garlic, crushed and finely chopped

1 tbsp of peeled and grated root ginger

2 dried Chinese mushrooms, soaked in hot water for 20 minutes, then drained and finely diced, or 2 shiitake mushrooms, sliced

1 small carrot, diced

250g (9oz) pork fillet, diced

1 tbsp of Shaoshing rice wine or dry sherry

50g (2oz) preserved mustard greens or gherkins, finely diced (or use diced courgette for a similar texture)

50g (2oz) dried Chinese wood ear mushrooms, soaked in hot water for 20 minutes, drained and finely chopped

125g (4½oz) tinned bamboo shoots, drained and diced

Handful of dry-roasted peanuts

2 tbsps of light soy sauce

1 tsp of toasted sesame oil

2–3 pinches of ground white pepper

1. Place the pancakes in a small bamboo steamer set over a saucepan of boiling water (making sure the bottom of the steamer doesn't touch the water) and steam for 5 minutes. Reduce the heat to low and keep the pancakes warm in the steamer until ready to serve.

2. Heat a wok over a medium heat until it starts to smoke and then add the groundnut oil. Add the garlic, ginger, Chinese or shiitake mushrooms and carrot and stir-fry together for just under a minute.

3. Add the pork and cook for 2–3 minutes or until it starts to turn brown, then stir in the rice wine or dry sherry.

4. Add the preserved mustard greens or gherkins, wood ear mushrooms, bamboo shoots and peanuts and mix well together. Finally, season with the soy sauce, toasted sesame oil and ground white pepper and serve wrapped in the steamed pancakes.

ALSO TRY
As an alternative to wheat-flour pancakes, use an iceberg lettuce instead: carefully peel away the leaves and use them as 'wraps', as served in Chinese takeaways and restaurants.

Chicken & Duck

When I stayed with my grandmother one summer in Taiwan, I witnessed her kill a live chicken. She did it ever so gently, making a small incision at the neck and draining the bird of its blood. I watched as the chicken's life ebbed swiftly away.

My grandmother collected the blood to make *ji xie gao* (literally 'chicken's blood cake'), in which the blood is mixed with pre-cooked glutinous rice and then moulded into rice cakes and grilled or wok-fried. It is a popular street snack. It also reflects a time when nothing of the bird was wasted – even its blood.

If only people were more in tune with their food today, as my grandparents were. I am a more thoughtful cook now; I always buy organic or free-range produce, I eat less meat and am very careful not to waste anything.

With the chicken offal, my grandmother would make a broth using the heart and kidneys, cooked with ginger and rice wine. Sometimes she would make a herbal soup; at other times she would blanch the offal and then steam it and serve it chopped up with a dressing of oil, ginger, chilli and spring onion. If there was any left over, she might then turn it into another dish by stir-frying it with leafy greens. Nothing was wasted and the whole bird would be eaten, even if it was through a few recycled meals. It didn't hurt us; the food always tasted delicious and was expertly prepared by an experienced cook.

The first time I witnessed the death of the chicken by my grandmother's hand, I couldn't quite bring myself to eat it. I had seen my uncle kill fish, so it should have been no different. But to see a chicken killed before my very eyes was a shock to the system. To liven my mood, my grandmother told me how, when my father and mother first got married, it was customary for the man to kill a chicken, to show his ability to look after his family. She said my father was useless at it. He had the whole family chasing after a headless chicken in the courtyard at his new in-laws' and was called a 'fake' farmer's son after that! When I confronted my father with the story, he said that the bird had been so strong, his hands had slipped and it escaped from his grip. Needless to say, his new bride was highly embarrassed and his father-in-law singularly unimpressed. I wasn't surprised that my father had never mentioned that incident!

My grandmother always gave thanks to the animals that sacrificed their lives for us and every month at the time of the full moon she would give up eating meat as a sign of respect. The way she lived – peacefully and gracefully, with respect for nature and the environment – inspires me so much. These are the principles that influence the way I live and eat today.

It is mostly chicken that features in the recipes in this section, reflecting the meat's popularity in the Chinese takeaway. Takeaway chicken is normally coated in a batter of egg white and cornflour, a process known as velveting. The chicken is then shallow-fried in oil and drained before being used in such favourites as General Tso's Chicken, or Kung Po Chicken (see pages 80 and 82). This technique keeps the meat lovely and tender and seals all the juices in. It is especially useful if you're cooking chicken breast, although I prefer to use thighs wherever possible because the meat is a lot juicier and more flavoursome.

My tip is to season the chicken with salt and ground white pepper and then dust it lightly with potato flour or cornflour before stir-frying it. Like velveting, this helps to seal the juices in but without having to shallow fry the meat, therefore keeping the dish healthier. This flour coating can sometimes catch on the side of the wok, but don't worry if it does – just keep stirring and tossing the chicken. You can cook the chicken pieces first before adding into the dish. It can also be helpful to add a dash of water to help the chicken move around in the wok.

Yellow bean chicken with French beans and shiitake mushrooms

Served with boiled jasmine rice, this makes a quick and delicious as well as highly nutritious supper.

PREP TIME: 10 minutes, plus 20 minutes for marinating
COOK IN: 10 minutes • **SERVES:** 2–4 to share

450g (1lb) skinless chicken breasts or thighs, sliced

2 tbsps of potato flour or cornflour

1 tbsp of groundnut oil

180g (6½oz) French beans, topped and tailed, then chopped into 4cm (1½in) pieces

4 shiitake mushrooms, stalks removed, then sliced

Salt and freshly ground pepper (optional)

2 small spring onions, finely chopped, to garnish

FOR THE MARINADE

2 cloves of garlic, crushed

1 tbsp of Shaohsing rice wine or dry sherry

1 tbsp of yellow bean paste

2 tbsps of light soy sauce

1 tbsp of runny honey

1. Mix together the ingredients for the marinade in a bowl, then add the chicken, turning it to coat in the mixture. Cover with cling film and leave to marinate for 20 minutes, then remove from the marinade and coat in the potato flour or cornflour.

2. Heat a wok over a high heat until the wok starts to smoke and then add the groundnut oil. Add the chicken and stir-fry for 4 minutes, then add the French beans and stir for 1 minute. Tip in the mushrooms and keep stirring for a further 1–2 minutes.

3. Check the seasoning, seasoning further to taste, if required. Sprinkle over the spring onions, then remove from the heat and serve immediately.

Chicken and black bean stir-fry

I adore fermented black beans and this is one of my favourite easy suppers. I add a touch of a good-quality yellow bean sauce for a savoury, mellow edge to the dish.

PREP TIME: 10 minutes • **COOK IN:** 5 minutes • **SERVES:** 2–4 to share

1 tbsp of groundnut oil

5 cloves of garlic, finely chopped

1 tbsp of peeled and grated root ginger

1 red chilli, deseeded and chopped

1 bird's eye chilli, deseeded and chopped

1 tbsp of fermented salted black beans, rinsed and crushed

450g (1lb) skinless chicken breasts or thighs, cut into 1cm (½in) slices

1 tbsp of Shaohsing rice wine or dry sherry

2 green peppers, deseeded and cut into chunks

200ml (7fl oz) vegetable stock

1 tbsp of light soy sauce

1 tbsp of cornflour mixed with 2 tbsps of water

1. Heat a wok over a high heat until it starts to smoke and then add the groundnut oil. Add the garlic, ginger and chillies and stir-fry for a few seconds, then add the fermented black beans and stir quickly.

2. Tip in the chicken slices and stir-fry for 1 minute, keeping the ingredients moving in the wok. As the meat starts to turn opaque, add the rice wine or dry sherry.

3. Add the green peppers and stir-fry for 1 minute, then add the stock and bring to the boil. Season with the soy sauce, then add the cornflour paste and stir to thicken. Serve immediately with jasmine rice.

General Tso's chicken

There are many variations of this recipe all over the world and it is particularly popular as a takeaway dish in America. Its inventor was from Hunan, a chef named Peng-Chang Kuei who fled with the Nationalist Party to Taiwan during the Second World War. Cooking for state banquets and official events for the Nationalist Party, he first came up with the dish in the 1950s, calling it after a Hunanese general from the Qing dynasty. Its original flavours were typically Hunanese – hot, sour, salty and heavy – but when he moved to New York in 1973, he adapted the recipe for the American palate. Peng was a friend of Henry Kissinger and it was he who is believed to have popularised Hunan cuisine in America. The dish's popularity has spread back to China where, ironically, Hunan chefs now claim it as a speciality of the region!

The taste should be sweet and spicy with a slight zing from the chillies – Sichuan sun-dried chillies if you can find them. You might be surprised by the use of ketchup; you can also use tomato purée if you prefer, adding a tiny bit of sugar.

PREP TIME: 5 minutes • **COOK IN:** 9 minutes • **SERVES:** 2–4 to share

2 skinless chicken breasts or 4 thighs, cut into 1.5cm (⅝in) cubes

Salt and ground white pepper

1 tbsp of potato flour or cornflour

1 tbsp of groundnut oil

1 clove of garlic, crushed

4 dried red chillies

1 tbsp of Shaohsing rice wine or dry sherry

4 spring onions, chopped into 2.5cm (1in) lengths

FOR THE SAUCE

1 tbsp of yellow bean sauce

1 tbsp of light soy sauce

1 tbsp of tomato ketchup

1 tbsp of chilli sauce

1 tsp of soft light brown sugar or runny honey

1 tsp of dark soy sauce

1. Place the chicken in a bowl and season with salt and pepper. Add the potato flour or cornflour and mix well. Place the ingredients for the sauce in another bowl and stir together.

2. Heat a wok over a high heat until it starts to smoke and then add the groundnut oil. Add the garlic and dried chillies and fry for a few seconds, then tip in the chicken pieces and stir-fry for 2 minutes. As the chicken starts to turn opaque, add the rice wine or dry sherry. Cook for another 2 minutes, then pour in the sauce and bring to the boil.

3. Cook the chicken in the sauce for a further 2 minutes or until it is cooked through and the sauce has reduced and thickened and is slightly sticky. Add the spring onions and cook for just under 1 minute, then transfer to a serving plate and serve immediately.

Kung Po chicken

This is a classic dish from Sichuan. It is named after Ding Baochen (1820–86), a governor of Sichuan; 'Gong Bao' or 'Kung Po' means 'palatial guardian', in reference to his official title. I love this spicy-sweet dish, but can't stand versions of it made with oyster sauce or cabbage. In my view, it should be numbingly spicy, sweet and tangy. There are many variations of the dish and this is my home-style Western version. The tang comes from the Chinkiang black rice vinegar.

PREP TIME: 10 minutes • **COOK IN:** 10 minutes • **SERVES:** 2–4 to share

2 skinless chicken breasts or 4 thighs, cut into 1cm (½in) slices

Salt and ground white pepper

1 tbsp of potato flour or cornflour

1 tbsp of groundnut oil

2 tbsps of Sichuan peppercorns

4 dried red chillies

1 tbsp of Shaohsing rice wine or dry sherry

1 red pepper, deseeded and cut into chunks

2 spring onions chopped into 2.5cm (1in) lengths

Handful of dry-roasted cashew nuts

FOR THE SAUCE

100ml (3½fl oz) cold vegetable stock

1 tbsp of light soy sauce

1 tbsp of tomato ketchup

1 tbsp of Chinkiang black rice vinegar or balsamic vinegar

1 tbsp of hoisin sauce

1 tsp of chilli sauce

1 tbsp of cornflour

1. Place the chicken in a bowl and season with salt and pepper. Add the potato flour or cornflour and mix well to coat the chicken pieces. Add all the ingredients for the sauce to another bowl and stir to combine.

2. Heat a wok over a high heat until it starts to smoke and then add the groundnut oil. Add the Sichuan peppercorns and dried chillies and fry for a few seconds, then add the chicken pieces and stir-fry for 2 minutes. As the chicken begins to turn opaque, add the rice wine or dry sherry. Cook for a further 2 minutes, then pour in the sauce.

3. Bring to the boil, add the red pepper and cook in the sauce with the chicken for another 2 minutes or until the meat is cooked through and the sauce has thickened and become slightly sticky in consistency. Add the spring onions and cook for 1 minute. Toss in the cashew nuts, then transfer to a serving plate and serve immediately.

> **CHING'S TIP**
> For a darker sauce, you could add a small drop of dark soy sauce.

Sichuan chilli tomato chicken

This dish brings together my two favourite ingredients. I love ripe heirloom tomatoes and I adore Sichuan peppercorns – their mouth-numbing spiciness is addictive.

PREP TIME: 10 minutes • **COOK IN:** 12 minutes • **SERVES:** 2–4 to share

1 tbsp of groundnut oil

2 cloves of garlic, crushed

1 tbsp of peeled and roughly sliced root ginger

1 red chilli, deseeded and finely chopped

1 tbsp of Sichuan peppercorns

1 tbsp of chilli bean paste

4 chicken thighs, deboned, and cut into 4cm (1½in) pieces

1 tbsp of Shaohsing rice wine or dry sherry

2 large ripe heirloom tomatoes or beef tomatoes, skin left on (see the tip below) and quartered

2 spring onions, cut on the diagonal into 2.5cm (1in) pieces

2 tbsps of cornflour mixed with 4 tbsps of water

FOR THE SAUCE

1 tbsp of light soy sauce

150ml (5fl oz) cold vegetable stock

1. Heat a wok over a high heat until it starts to smoke and then add the groundnut oil. Add the garlic, ginger, chilli, Sichuan peppercorns and chilli bean paste and stir well for just under a minute.

2. Add the chicken pieces and keep stirring until they start to turn opaque. Pour in the rice wine or dry sherry and cook for about 4 minutes, stirring continuously, then add the tomatoes and stir to combine.

3. Pour in the sauce ingredients, then bring to the boil and cook for 4 minutes or until the chicken is cooked through. Tip in the spring onions and cook for 1 minute or until softened. Thicken the sauce with the cornflour paste, then transfer to a plate and serve immediately, accompanied with jasmine rice.

> **CHING'S TIP**
> There's no need to skin the tomatoes – the skin holds all the nutrients. If you want to skin them, however, see the tip on page 30.

Steamed chicken with Chinese mushrooms, goji berries and dried lily bulbs

My grandmother used to prepare a similar dish to this on special occasions to which she would add dried Chinese dates and bamboo shoots. This is my recreation of her recipe: the goji berries add sweetness and the lily bulbs give fragrance. Serve with jasmine rice.

PREP TIME: 10 minutes • **COOK IN:** 20 minutes • **SERVES:** 2

1 tbsp of groundnut oil

2 tbsps of Shaohsing rice wine or dry sherry

1 tbsp of toasted sesame oil

2 chicken thighs, skinned and each piece halved on the bone (or use skinless, boneless chicken thighs)

2.5cm (1in) piece of root ginger, peeled and sliced

2 dried Chinese mushrooms, soaked in hot water for 20 minutes, then drained and sliced, or 2 shiitake mushrooms, sliced

Salt and ground white pepper

30g (1¼oz) dried lily bulbs, soaked in warm water for 20 minutes, then drained

Handful of dried goji berries, soaked in warm water for 20 minutes, then drained

1. Combine the groundnut oil, rice wine or dry sherry and toasted sesame oil in a bowl. Add the chicken, ginger and sliced Chinese or shiitake mushrooms. Season with salt and pepper, then toss all the ingredients together and arrange on a small heatproof plate.

2. Lay the lily bulbs on top of the chicken and sprinkle with the goji berries, then place the plate inside a bamboo steamer. Set the steamer over a small pan of boiling water (making sure the bottom of the steamer doesn't touch the water) and steam on a high heat for 20 minutes. Use a skewer to check that the chicken is cooked through, then remove from the heat and serve immediately.

Oyster-sauce chicken with ginger and shiitake mushrooms

This is one of my own flavour combinations, inspired by southern Chinese dishes from regions such as Canton and Fujian, where the combination of meat and seafood is very common. I hope you like it!

PREP TIME: 10 minutes • **COOK IN:** 9 minutes • **SERVES:** 2–4 to share

2 chicken thighs and 3 drumsticks (500g/1lb 2oz in total), skinned and the meatier parts sliced off but keeping some of the flesh on the bone (or use skinless, boneless chicken thighs)

Salt and ground white pepper

1 tbsp of potato flour or cornflour

1 tbsp of groundnut oil

2.5cm (1in) piece of root ginger, peeled and sliced

1 tbsp of Shaohsing rice wine or dry sherry

5 shiitake mushrooms, sliced

2 large spring onions, sliced on the diagonal

FOR THE SAUCE

1 tbsp of light soy sauce

1 tbsp of oyster sauce

1 tbsp of chilli sauce

100ml (3½fl oz) cold vegetable stock

1. Place the chicken pieces in a bowl and season with salt and pepper. Add the potato flour or cornflour and mix well to coat the chicken. Pour all the ingredients for the sauce into another bowl and stir together to combine.

2. Heat a wok over a high heat until it starts to smoke and add the groundnut oil. Add the ginger and fry for a few seconds, then add the chicken pieces and stir-fry for 4 minutes, stirring constantly.

3. As the chicken starts to turn opaque, add the rice wine or dry sherry and cook for a further 2 minutes, then add the sauce and bring to the boil. Tip in the shiitake mushrooms and cook for 1 minute, then stir in the spring onions. Remove from the heat and serve immediately.

Hoisin chicken

This recipe uses shop-bought hoisin sauce to make a delicious marinade for coating the chicken before roasting it in the oven. The sweet flavour goes down well with children and makes it perfect as an accompaniment to other, saltier-tasting dishes. Great for a barbecue on a hot day, this is equally suitable for making at any time of year.

PREP TIME: 5 minutes, plus 20 minutes for marinating
COOK IN: 32 minutes • **SERVES:** 2–4 to share

2 chicken thighs and 3 drumsticks (500g/1lb 2oz in total), skin on

1 spring onion, finely sliced, to garnish

FOR THE MARINADE

1 tbsp of Shaohsing rice wine or dry sherry

2 tbsps of hoisin sauce

4 tbsps of light soy sauce

1 tbsp of dark soy sauce

1 tbsp of soft light brown sugar

1 tbsp of groundnut oil

2.5cm (1in) piece of root ginger, peeled and grated

1. Place all the marinade ingredients in a large bowl, then add the chicken pieces and toss in the marinade to coat. Cover the bowl with cling film and place in the fridge to marinate for at least 20 minutes.

2. Meanwhile, preheat the oven to 180°C (350°F), gas mark 4.

3. Remove the chicken pieces from the marinade (retaining the liquid) and place in a roasting tin. Roast in the oven for 30 minutes or until cooked through and crispy on top.

4. Just before serving, pour the marinade into a small saucepan, bring to the boil and drizzle over the chicken. Sprinkle over the spring onion and serve with rice and salad or vegetables, such as the Pak Choy with Carrot and Garlic (see page 144).

Twice-cooked salt and pepper chicken

This is one of my favourite ways to cook a whole chicken. Organic is best, as there is less fat beneath the skin – the trick to getting a deliciously crisp skin. The chicken is first stuffed and boiled to infuse all the flavours, then roasted until the skin is golden.

PREP TIME: 20 minutes • **COOK IN:** 1 hour 40 minutes • **SERVES:** 4

1 x 2kg (4lb 4oz) chicken

10cm (4in) piece of root ginger, peeled and sliced

4 spring onions, cut into 2.5cm (1in) slices, white and green parts separated

5 dried Chinese mushrooms, soaked in hot water for 20 minutes, then drained and sliced, or 5 shiitake mushrooms, sliced

3 star anise

1 tbsp of Sichuan peppercorns

1 tsp of salt

¼ tsp of ground white pepper

2 tbsps of Shaohsing rice wine or dry sherry

300g (11oz) jasmine rice

FOR THE SPICE RUB

1 tsp of sea salt

1 tsp of ground white pepper

1 tbsp of Chinese five-spice powder

1 tbsp of groundnut oil

1. Wash the chicken thoroughly and pat dry with kitchen paper, then stuff the cavity with the ginger, the white parts of the spring onions and the mushrooms.

2. Bring 2.5 litres (4⅓ pints) of water to the boil in a large saucepan or casserole. Put in the chicken with the star anise, Sichuan peppercorns, salt, pepper and rice wine or dry sherry. Bring back to the boil, then reduce the heat to medium and simmer, uncovered, for 1 hour, removing any scum that rises to the surface.

3. Add the green parts of the spring onions and cook for a further 20 minutes, then remove the chicken and drain well, retaining the stock.

4. Preheat the oven to 220°C (425°F), gas mark 7. Mix together the ingredients for the spice rub, then brush over the skin of the chicken. Place in a roasting tin and roast in the oven for 15 minutes or until the skin is crispy and golden.

5. Meanwhile, rinse the rice and place in a saucepan. Pour in 600ml (1 pint) of the retained chicken stock and bring to the boil. Reduce to low, cover and simmer for 20 minutes or until the rice has absorbed the stock and is cooked and fluffy.

6. Remove the chicken from the oven and allow to rest. Carve and serve with the rice and a dipping sauce of olive oil mixed with chopped ginger, chillies and spring onions.

Three-cup chicken

This Taiwanese recipe is so called because it uses 1 cup of soy sauce, 1 cup of toasted sesame oil and 1 cup of rice wine. You can vary the amounts, but the final dish should be slightly sticky.

PREP TIME: 10 minutes • **COOK IN:** 14 minutes • **SERVES:** 2–4 to share

1 tbsp of groundnut oil

5 cloves of garlic, finely chopped

2.5cm (1in) piece of root ginger, peeled and sliced

4 chicken thighs, skin on, deboned and cut into 4cm (1½in) pieces

50ml (2fl oz) light soy sauce

50ml (2fl oz) toasted sesame oil

50ml (2fl oz) Shaohsing rice wine or dry sherry

1 tbsp of soft light brown sugar

Small handful of Chinese basil leaves, or Thai or Italian sweet basil, plus extra to garnish

1 red chilli, deseeded and cut into strips, to garnish (optional)

1. Heat a wok over a high heat until it starts to smoke and then add the groundnut oil. Add the garlic and ginger and stir-fry for a few seconds, then add the chicken and stir-fry for 2–3 minutes or until it has browned. Add the soy sauce, toasted sesame oil and rice wine or dry sherry and cook on a medium heat for 6 minutes. Stir well and add the sugar.

2. Bring to the boil, then reduce the heat and simmer for about 5 minutes or until the sauce has reduced completely and the chicken is cooked through. Remove from the heat, stir in the basil leaves and leave to wilt slightly.

3. Pour on to a serving plate, garnish with the chilli strips if you like, and more basil leaves and serve immediately with some jasmine rice.

> **CHING'S TIP**
> Since you want a dry stir-fry here, it's important to use toasted sesame oil, which will reduce as it cooks, and not pure sesame oil, which will just keep on cooking and not reduce.

Chilli chicken and cashew nuts

The traditional technique for making this dish involves three or four stages. However, I have adapted the recipe so that the chicken is cooked in no time, giving you a tasty meal in minutes.

PREP TIME: 10 minutes • **COOK IN:** 7 minutes • **SERVES:** 2

3 chicken thighs, skinned, deboned and cut into 2cm (¾in) chunks (or use skinless, boneless chicken thighs)

1 tsp of potato flour or cornflour mixed with 1 tbsp of water

½ tsp of Chinese five-spice powder

2 tbsps of groundnut oil

1 tsp of Sichuan peppercorns

1 tsp of chilli bean paste

1 red chilli, deseeded and ground using a pestle and mortar

Dash of Shaohsing rice wine or dry sherry

100g (3½oz) roasted salted cashew nuts

2 spring onions, sliced on the diagonal

1 tsp of light soy sauce, or to taste

½ lime

1. Place the chicken pieces in a bowl, add the potato flour or cornflour paste and turn to coat, then season with the five-spice powder.

2. Heat a wok over a high heat until it starts to smoke and add the groundnut oil. Add the Sichuan peppercorns, chilli bean paste and ground red chilli and stir-fry for 30 seconds.

3. Tip in the chicken pieces and leave to settle in the wok for 30 seconds, then add the rice wine or dry sherry. Toss all the ingredients together and cook for 3–4 minutes or until the chicken has turned virtually opaque.

4. Add the cashew nuts and cook for another minute, then add the spring onions, toss well and cook for a further minute. Season to taste with the soy sauce and add a squeeze of lime juice. Divide between plates and serve with egg-fried rice or plain rice.

Fruity sweet and sour duck

The Cantonese are known for their love of sweet and sour combinations and this recipe comes from that region. It's a home-style dish – easy, fruity and ready in minutes. I hope you enjoy it.

PREP TIME: 15 minutes • **COOK IN:** 5 minutes • **SERVES:** 2

2 x 250g (9oz) duck breasts, skinned and cut into thin slices

Sea salt and ground white pepper

1 tsp of Shaohsing rice wine or dry sherry

2 tbsps of potato flour or cornflour

200ml (7fl oz) groundnut oil

2.5cm (1in) piece of root ginger, peeled and finely sliced

1 red pepper, deseeded and cut into 1cm (½in) chunks

50g (2oz) peeled pineapple, cut into 1.5cm (⅝in) cubes

Juice of 2 small oranges

Juice of 1 lime

1 tbsp of light soy sauce

Few orange segments, to garnish

1. Put the slices of duck breast into a bowl with some salt, white pepper, the rice wine or dry sherry and the potato flour or cornflour and mix well.

2. Place a wok over a high heat and add the groundnut oil. Heat the oil to 180°C (350°F) or until a cube of bread dropped in turns golden brown in 15 seconds and floats to the surface. Using a slotted spoon, add the duck and shallow-fry for about 2 minutes or until crispy on the outside.

3. Take the wok off the heat, remove the duck from the hot oil and drain on kitchen paper. Pour the oil from the wok through a sieve into a heatproof container and save to use later.

4. Set the wok back over a high heat until it starts to smoke and then add 1 tbsp of the retained groundnut oil. Add the ginger and stir-fry for a few seconds, then add the red pepper and pineapple and stir-fry for a further minute. Return the duck to the wok, season with the orange juice, lime juice and soy sauce and toss well.

5. Garnish with orange segments and serve immediately with Egg and Asparagus Fried Rice (see page 186).

Beef, Pork & Lamb

When I was growing up, meat was a luxury. We never ate lamb and beef was expensive and rare, so the meat most often served at our kitchen table was pork or chicken and sometimes duck (usually on a special occasion). Pork was and still is the meat most commonly eaten in a Chinese household. My father used to breed pigs for sale because it made money; he would never eat them and so grew up rarely eating pork. He would always say to us (and still does), 'Do you know how lucky you are? All we had for breakfast was cold leftover rice with soy sauce!' Occasionally it would be cold roast sweet potatoes instead, if he was lucky. He was one of eight children and mealtimes were a fight between him and his siblings. He was the lucky one, relatively speaking, because he was the eldest son and therefore the most treasured in the family, so he usually got more than the others.

Traditionally, pork was the most commonly consumed type of meat in China because dishes could be created using the whole animal. The pig's ears would be dried in the sun, then rehydrated and cooked in stir-fries. Its trotters would be stewed. The legs, shoulder and fillet would be roasted, while the belly meat would be slow-cooked in a spiced soy stewing liquid and eaten with rice. Any leftover pork fat would be used to make dried pork sausages. The pig's heart and kidneys were used in broths or stir-fried, and the intestines stir-fried with ginger and rice wine or sometimes served with a chilli sauce. Rice wine helped to kill any bacteria and mask any odours of meat that was past its best. My father said his favourite was the pig's tail, slow-cooked until the skin was so tender that it melted in the mouth.

It was only when I moved to South Africa from Taiwan that I began to eat, and enjoy, beef and lamb.

I remember on my first day at school being given a toasted minced beef sandwich with ketchup. It was the most delicious thing I had ever tasted, made all the more special by being given to me by Lindsay, my first school friend.

South Africans are well known for their love of braais (barbecues), and as I learned the way of life there, I attended many braai parties. I was introduced to different ways of eating and different cuts of meat like sirloin steak and racks of lamb. I also tried my first biltong (dried beef jerky), which became my favourite snack, as well as *boerewors* ('farmer's sausage'). Some were made with different herbs and seasonings; those made with pork fat were called *spekwors*. I also tried *droe-wors*, a type of dried sausage – much drier than, for example, salami. I also had gamey meat like ostrich and springbok. It was all so delicious – like being in meat heaven! This was such a different world from growing up in Taiwan, and if I thought I was in meat heaven, my father must have thought he was in paradise!

There is no shortage of meat on a takeaway menu, of course. Takeaway chefs know how to get the best out of the meat by using bones to make stock or tenderising and marinating cheaper cuts to be used in delicious stir-fries. However, the beauty of creating your own takeaway experience at home is that you can be more extravagant if you prefer. I have included some takeaway classics but with a twist, such as Beef in Oyster Sauce with Choy Sum, Chilli Peanut Beef and Cantonese-style Sweet and Sour Pork (see pages 100, 101 and 108). Most can be prepared within 30 minutes and are perfect for a midweek supper or for entertaining friends and family.

Beef in oyster sauce with choy sum

This makes a great instant supper for serving on a weekday – a classic takeaway dish that's also perfect for cooking at home. Eat it carb-free or serve with rice.

PREP TIME: 10 minutes • **COOK IN:** 5 minutes • **SERVES:** 2

350g (12oz) beef fillet
2 tbsps of groundnut oil

FOR THE MARINADE
1 tsp of light soy sauce
1 tbsp of oyster sauce
Pinch of soft light brown
    sugar
Pinch of salt
Pinch of ground black pepper

FOR THE CHOY SUM
3 cloves of garlic, crushed and
    finely chopped
1 red chilli, deseeded and
    finely chopped
200g (7oz) choy sum, sliced
    into 6cm (2½in) lengths
Pinch of salt
1 tsp of oyster sauce

1. Prepare the beef fillet by tenderising it with a meat hammer or the side of a Chinese cleaver. Slice it thinly and place the pieces in a bowl along with all the ingredients for the marinade. Stir in the marinade to coat and then set aside while you cook the choy sum.

2. Heat a wok over a high heat until it starts to smoke and then add half the groundnut oil. Add the garlic and chilli and toss together quickly, then add the choy sum and mix in. Add a drop of water to help create some steam to cook the vegetables, then stir-fry for 1 minute. Season with the salt and the oyster sauce and transfer to a warmed serving plate.

3. Place the wok back over a high heat and add the remaining groundnut oil. Tip in the beef slices and stir-fry for 1–2 minutes. Place on top of the cooked choy sum and serve immediately.

Chilli peanut beef

This dish is spicy and mouth-tinglingly delicious with a capital D. It's quick and easy to cook too!

PREP TIME: 5 minutes • **COOK IN:** 5 minutes • **SERVES:** 2–4 to share

250g (9oz) beef fillet
1 tbsp of groundnut oil
2 dried red chillies
1 tbsp of Sichuan peppercorns
1 tbsp of Shaohsing rice wine or dry sherry
Dash of chilli oil
Dash of toasted sesame oil
Handful of dry-roasted peanuts
Small handful of coriander, finely chopped (optional)

FOR THE SAUCE
1 tbsp of chilli bean paste
1 tbsp of crunchy peanut butter
1 tbsp of light soy sauce
1 tbsp of Chinkiang black rice vinegar or balsamic vinegar
1 tbsp of cornflour

1. Prepare the beef fillet by tenderising it with a meat hammer or the side of a Chinese cleaver, then slice it into thin strips.

2. Heat a wok over a high heat until it starts to smoke and then add the groundnut oil. Add the Sichuan peppercorns and dried chillies and toss together for a few seconds, then tip in the slices of beef fillet and stir-fry for 30 seconds. As the meat starts to turn brown, add the rice wine or dry sherry.

3. Mix together the ingredients for the sauce and add to the wok, stirring well to combine with the beef, then bring to the boil.

4. Remove from the heat and drizzle over a little chilli oil and toasted sesame oil. Add the peanuts and coriander (if using) and toss together to combine, then transfer to a serving plate and serve immediately with rice and Special Mixed Vegetables (see page 155).

Beef with bean sprouts and spring onions

If you want a tasty, effortless supper, then you can't get any easier than this dish. A short time marinating, then speedy cooking in a hot wok ensures that dinner is on the table in no time. While the beef is marinating, you can boil some rice or, better still, make it in a rice cooker if you have one.

PREP TIME: 10 minutes, plus 20 minutes for marinating • **COOK IN:** 4 minutes • **SERVES:** 2

250g (9oz) beef sirloin, fat removed and meat cut into 1cm (½in) slices

1 tbsp of groundnut oil

150g (5oz) bean sprouts or soya bean sprouts

1 tsp of cornflour mixed with 1 tbsp of water

2 spring onions, finely chopped

FOR THE MARINADE

2 cloves of garlic, crushed

2 tbsps of peeled and grated ginger

2 tbsps of light soy sauce

1 tsp of dark soy sauce

1 tsp of soft light brown sugar

2 tbsps of mirin

1. Place all the marinade ingredients in a large bowl, then add the beef slices and mix well to coat. Cover the bowl with cling film and set the beef aside to marinate for 20 minutes.

2. Heat a wok over a high heat until it starts to smoke and then add the groundnut oil. Remove the beef from the bowl, retaining the marinade, and cook for 2 minutes.

3. Add the bean sprouts, reserved marinade and the cornflour paste, then toss together and cook for a further minute. Stir in the finely chopped spring onions, transfer to a serving plate and serve immediately with jasmine rice.

Black pepper beef and rainbow vegetable stir-fry

My grandmother always said that if we ate vegetables of every colour of the rainbow, we would stay as healthy as anything. This is the perfect way to ensure you get more than your five a day.

PREP TIME: 10 minutes, plus 20 minutes for marinating • **COOK IN:** 5 minutes • **SERVES:** 2–4

250g (9oz) beef sirloin, fat removed and meat cut into 5mm (¼in) slices

1 tbsp of cornflour

2 tbsps of groundnut oil

2.5cm (1in) piece of root ginger, peeled and grated

300g (11oz) mix of sliced mangetout, broccoli, sugar snap peas, baby pak choy, red cabbage, ribbons of carrot and baby spring onions

Dash of light soy sauce or to taste

FOR THE MARINADE

1 tbsp of dark soy sauce

1 tbsp of light soy sauce

1 tbsp of Shaohsing rice wine or dry sherry

2 pinches of ground black pepper

1. Mix together the ingredients for the marinade in a large bowl, then add the beef and stir to coat. Cover the bowl with cling film and set aside for 20 minutes to marinate, then remove from the marinade (retaining this) and dust with the cornflour.

2. Heat a wok over a high heat, and when it starts to smoke, add half the groundnut oil. Add the ginger and stir-fry for a second or so, then add the vegetable mix and toss together in the wok. Add a drop of water to create a little steam for cooking the vegetables. Cook for 1 minute and transfer to a plate.

3. Place the wok back over the heat and add the remaining groundnut oil, followed by the beef. Let the meat settle for a few seconds, then stir in the wok for 1–2 minutes. Tip in the stir-fried vegetables and toss together with the beef. Season further, to taste, with light soy sauce, then transfer to a serving plate and eat immediately.

Xi'an-style beef curry in a hurry

Xi'an was the ancient capital of China and marked the end of the Silk Road, along which many spices found their way into the country. In the markets in central Xi'an, stalls still sell a huge array of spices, used to create a variety of spicy dishes, including curries.

Curry in one form or another is eaten throughout the country, so it is no surprise that it has a place on the Chinese takeaway menu. Curry flavours will vary from place to place, but the spices almost always include turmeric, mild curry powder, dried chillies and garam masala. This is my version of a Xi'an-style beef curry, with new potatoes, carrots and peas to add sweetness and texture.

PREP TIME: 10 minutes • **COOK IN:** 10 minutes • **SERVES:** 2–4 to share

3 new potatoes (400g/14oz in total), peeled and cut into 1cm (½in) chunks

1 carrot (100g/3½oz), cut into 1cm (½in) chunks

300g (11oz) beef sirloin, cut into 2cm (¾in) chunks

1 tsp of turmeric

1 tsp of medium curry powder

Pinch of salt

Pinch of ground white pepper

1 tbsp of groundnut oil

1 white onion, diced

1 star anise

1 tbsp of Shaohsing rice wine or dry sherry

100g (3½oz) frozen peas

FOR THE SAUCE

1 tbsp of light soy sauce

1 tbsp of dark soy sauce

100ml (3½fl oz) cold chicken stock

2 tbsps of cornflour

1. Place the potatoes and carrots in a saucepan of water, bring to the boil and keep boiling for 5 minutes. Remove from the heat, drain and refresh in cold water, then set aside.

2. Place the beef in a large bowl along with the turmeric, curry powder and salt and pepper, and stir the meat in the spices to coat.

3. Heat a wok over a high heat until it starts to smoke and then add the groundnut oil. Tip in the onion and stir-fry until translucent, then add the star anise and the seasoned beef pieces. As the beef starts to turn brown at the edges, add the rice wine or dry sherry.

4. Pour in the ingredients for the sauce and bring to boil, then add the parboiled potatoes and carrot, followed by the peas, and bring back up to boil. Reduce the heat to medium and simmer for 2–3 minutes, then serve immediately with jasmine rice.

Cantonese-style sweet and sour pork

You will recognise this sweet and sour pork recipe as similar to that served in the Chinese restaurants in the UK. However, some can be sickly sweet and the batter quite thick. This is my healthier and lighter version.

PREP TIME: 15 minutes • **COOK IN:** 12 minutes • **SERVES:** 2–4 to share

1 egg, beaten

1 tbsp of cornflour

250g (9oz) pork fillet, cut into 5mm (¼in) slices

Salt and ground white pepper

400ml (14fl oz) groundnut oil

2.5cm (1in) piece of root ginger, peeled and grated

1 red pepper, deseeded and cut into chunks

1 green pepper, deseeded and cut into chunks

1 x 227g tin of pineapple chunks in juice, sliced

1 tbsp of light soy sauce

1 tbsp of clear rice vinegar or cider vinegar

½ tsp of soft light brown sugar (optional)

1 tsp of cornflour mixed with 1 tbsp of water

1. Mix the egg and cornflour together in a large bowl to make a batter. Stir the pork fillet slices in the mixture, seasoning with salt and pepper.

2. Place a wok over a high heat and add the groundnut oil. Heat the oil to 180°C (350°F) or until a cube of bread dropped in turns golden brown in 15 seconds and floats to the surface. Carefully lower the pork slices into the oil and fry for 3–4 minutes or until golden brown. Lift out using tongs or a slotted spoon and place on a plate lined with kitchen paper to drain any excess oil.

3. Sieve the oil into a heatproof container and save to use later. Retain 1 tbsp of the oil in the wok and heat until it starts to smoke. Add the grated ginger and the peppers and quickly stir in the wok to stop the ginger from catching. Stir for 2 minutes, then add the sliced pineapple chunks and their juice from the tin and bring to the boil.

4. Season with the soy sauce, vinegar and brown sugar (if using), then as the liquid in the wok reduces and boils, thicken with the cornflour paste. Tip the fried pork back into the wok, stirring and tossing together so that it is covered in the sauce. Remove from the heat and serve immediately with boiled rice and stir-fried vegetables.

Yin and yang crispy pork salad

The pork in this dish is marinated and fried, then served on a bed of fresh Little Gem lettuce leaves. Simple, delicious, well balanced and full of flavour.

PREP TIME: 10 minutes, plus 20 minutes for marinating • **COOK IN:** 3 minutes • **SERVES:** 2

250g (9oz) pork fillet, cut into 5mm (¼in) slices

400ml (14fl oz) groundnut oil

50g (2oz) potato flour or cornflour

FOR THE MARINADE

1 tbsp of peeled and grated ginger

1 tbsp of Shaohsing rice wine or dry sherry

1 spring onion, finely chopped

1 tsp of Sichuan peppercorns, toasted and ground (see the tip on page 49)

½ tsp of salt

1 tsp of light soy sauce

1 tsp of yellow bean sauce

1 tsp of hoisin sauce

Pinch of Chinese five-spice powder

TO SERVE

1 tbsp of sesame seeds, toasted (see the tip on page 44)

Little Gem lettuce leaves, sliced

1 spring onion, finely sliced

1. Mix the marinade ingredients together in a large bowl, add the pork and stir to coat, then cover in cling film, place in the fridge and leave to marinate for a minimum of 20 minutes or preferably overnight.

2. Place a wok over a high heat and add the groundnut oil. Heat the oil to 180°C (350°F) or until a cube of bread dropped into the oil turns golden brown in 15 seconds and floats to the surface.

3. Dust the pork pieces in the potato flour or cornflour and then place in the hot oil, frying for 2–3 minutes or until golden brown. Lift the pieces out using tongs or a slotted spoon and then drain on kitchen paper.

4. To serve, dress the serving plate with a bed of sliced Little Gem leaves, then place the pork slices on top, sprinkle over the toasted sesame seeds and scatter with the sliced spring onion.

Black bean wok-fried ribs with bean sprouts and chillies

This tasty stir-fry uses chunky short ribs to allow for quick wok cooking. Fermented black beans and chillies add smoky and spicy flavours. It's perfect served with stir-fried vegetables and rice.

PREP TIME: 5 minutes • **COOK IN:** 10 minutes • **SERVES:** 2–4 to share

1 tbsp of groundnut oil

2 cloves of garlic, crushed

1 red chilli, deseeded and finely chopped

1 tbsp fermented salted black beans, rinsed and crushed

250g (9oz) pork ribs, chopped into 2.5cm (1in) pieces

1 tbsp of Shaohsing rice wine or dry sherry

Large handful of bean sprouts

1 tbsp of light soy sauce

1 tbsp of dark soy sauce

1 green chilli, sliced

1. Heat a wok over a high heat until it starts to smoke and then add the groundnut oil. Add the garlic and red chilli and stir quickly for a few seconds, then add the beans and stir for a few more seconds.

2. Tip in the pork ribs and stir-fry for 1 minute, then add the rice wine or dry sherry. Cook the ribs for 6 minutes or until browned, stirring continuously and adding a small dash of water to help cook the meat. Add the bean sprouts and both the light and dark soy sauce.

3. Stir in the sliced green chillies and cook until the bean sprouts have wilted slightly but still retain a crunch. Remove from the heat and serve immediately.

Red-cooked bacon lardons, shiitake mushrooms and chestnuts

Whenever winter draws in, I find myself craving stews and braised dishes. I love the 'red-cooking' technique (referring to the colour of the cooking liquid) and like to use it to create new dishes. For this recipe, I've used it for cooking bacon coupled with my favourite, earthy shiitake mushrooms and sweet, nutty roasted chestnuts. This is a dish that will keep your stomach warm and happy however cold it is outside.

PREP TIME: 5 minutes • **COOK IN:** 7 minutes • **SERVES:** 2–4 to share

1 tbsp of groundnut oil

1 tbsp of Chinese five spice (whole spices)

100g (3½oz) bacon, cut into lardons

1 tbsp of Shaohsing rice wine or dry sherry

1 tbsp of light soy sauce

1 tsp of dark soy sauce

1 tbsp of soft light brown sugar

4 shiitake mushrooms, sliced

10 peeled and ready-roasted chestnuts

2 spring onions, sliced, to garnish

1. Heat a wok over a high heat until it starts to smoke and then add the groundnut oil. Add the whole spices and stir for a few seconds, then tip in the bacon lardons and cook for 1 minute or until fragrant and browned.

2. Pour in the rice wine or dry sherry and the light and dark soy sauce and add the sugar. Add the mushrooms and chestnuts and bring to the boil, stirring continuously.

3. When the liquid has reduced and the ingredients are slightly sticky with the red glaze, remove from the heat and garnish with the spring onions. Serve immediately with some jasmine rice.

Fish-fragrant aubergine with pork

This is my take on a classic Sichuan aubergine dish (*yu xiang qiezi*) in which 'fish-fragrant' is used to describe the savoury smell of the stock. Traditionally the aubergine is 'passed through the oil', i.e. shallow-fried, to give it a silken creamy texture. I've stir-fried it here, for a healthier option. I have also added minced pork and Sichuan peppercorns for a comforting winter dish that can be cooked in minutes.

PREP TIME: 10 minutes • **COOK IN:** 10 minutes • **SERVES:** 2–4 to share

2 tbsps of groundnut oil

1 aubergine (about 200g/7oz), sliced into batons

2 cloves of garlic, crushed and finely chopped

2.5cm (1in) piece of root ginger, peeled and grated

1 red chilli, deseeded and finely chopped

1 tbsp of Sichuan peppercorns

250g (9oz) lean minced pork

1 tbsp of Shaohsing rice wine or dry sherry

2 spring onions, cut on the diagonal into 2.5cm (1in) slices

Salt and ground white pepper

FOR THE SAUCE

100ml (3½fl oz) vegetable stock

1 tbsp of light soy sauce

1 tbsp Chinkiang black rice vinegar or balsamic vinegar

1 tbsp of cornflour

1. Heat a wok over a high heat until it starts to smoke and then pour in half the groundnut oil. Add the aubergine pieces and stir-fry for about 5 minutes or until browned, adding a dash of water now and then to soften the aubergine. Once it is cooked, transfer to a plate.

2. Reheat the wok and add the remaining groundnut oil. Add the garlic, ginger, chilli and Sichuan peppercorns and stir-fry for a few seconds, then add the pork, breaking it up in the wok with a wooden spoon. As the pork starts to turn brown, add the rice wine or dry sherry and cook for 2 minutes.

3. Add the cooked aubergine to the pork, then pour in the sauce ingredients and bring to the boil. Reduce the heat, then add the spring onions and cook for just under a minute or until softened. Season further, to taste, with salt and pepper and serve immediately with jasmine or brown rice.

Spicy lamb stew

This classic Chinese dish brings together spices from central China, chilli bean paste from Sichuan, potatoes from the New World and carrots from Europe – fusion cooking before the term was invented, you might say! Delicious and easy to make, it tastes even better if kept and eaten on the following day. Serve with mantou (Chinese-style steamed buns), pitta bread or buttered rolls.

PREP TIME: 10 minutes, plus 20 minutes for marinating
COOK IN: 1 hour • **SERVES:** 2–4 to share

400g (14oz) lamb steak, cut into 1.5cm (⅝in) cubes

200g (7oz) new potatoes, peeled and cut into 2cm (¾in) chunks

100g (3½oz) carrots, cut into 2cm (¾in) chunks

2 tbsps of groundnut oil

2 shallots, diced

2 star anise

1 tbsp of Shaohsing rice wine or dry sherry

1 tbsp of chilli bean paste

600ml (1 pint) vegetable stock

1 tbsp of cornflour mixed with 1 tbsp of water

FOR THE SPICE PASTE

¼ tsp of hot chilli powder

1 tsp of ground cumin

1 tsp of turmeric

1 tsp of medium curry powder

1 tsp of fennel seeds

1 tbsp of groundnut oil

1. Mix together the ingredients for the spice paste in a large bowl, then add the lamb and stir to coat. Cover with cling film and leave to marinate for 20 minutes.

2. Meanwhile, place the potatoes and carrots in a saucepan of water, bring to the boil and keep boiling for 7 minutes. Remove from the heat, drain and refresh under cold water, then set aside.

3. Heat a wok over a high heat until it starts to smoke and then add the groundnut oil. Add the shallots and star anise and stir-fry for 2 minutes. Tip in the marinated lamb chunks and stir-fry until they start to turn brown.

4. Add the rice wine or dry sherry and cook for 2 minutes, then add the chilli bean paste and stir-fry for a few seconds. Pour in the stock and bring to the boil, then reduce the heat to medium and cook, uncovered, for 40 minutes. Add the parboiled potatoes and carrots and cook for another 5 minutes, then stir in the cornflour paste to thicken the stew and serve immediately.

Fish &
Shellfish

When we lived in Taiwan, a small grey-haired woman would ride by on her large bicycle with a bucket attached to the front. Wearing a tall pointed hat of woven bamboo and a large red handkerchief tied across her face, she would ring her bell whenever she passed my grandparents' home.

The dirty white bucket would be full of water with some small river fish or sometimes live farmed carp swimming around in it. Depending on what was in the bucket and what she had decided to cook that day, my grandmother would always buy something from the fish woman if she could.

When my parents came to visit us or when we had special guests, my grandmother would always cook fish. It was expensive and, after chicken or duck, the most prized form of meat. We hardly ever ate beef because cattle were bred for sale and oxen used for working the land.

My grandmother's favourite ways of preparing fish were either steamed or wok-fried with ginger and soy sauce. The fish was almost always served whole unless she had a craving for fish-head soup, in which case it would be chopped up and cooked in a broth with ginger, coriander and dofu.

There is a real etiquette to eating fish. Usually the best bits, including the head and belly, would be served to the elders first and then, as youngsters, we would be given the tail and leftovers. We were never allowed to turn the fish over: one side would be eaten and then the skeleton moved to one side before the lower fillet was touched. There is the Chinese superstition that if you turn the fish over, you will miss a journey or cause a boat to capsize! Whatever the case, nothing of the fish went to waste.

My grandmother would serve good-sized portions of fish for me and my brother, but he used to hate fish and would secretly put his portion inside my bowl when grandmother wasn't looking. My grandmother used to tell us that if you ate fish, you would be as clever and quick as a fish, and I believed her so always ate what I was given. Whenever my brother bullied me, I used to retaliate by telling him that I was cleverer than him because I ate fish and he didn't.

In Chinese culture, a fish is a symbol of wealth and fortune because the word for fish, *yu*, is also a homonym for wealth and abundance. At Chinese New Year, it is customary to use the phrase '*Nian nian you yu*' ('May you have great abundance every year'). That is why you see fish appearing on posters and decorations for Chinese New Year.

I didn't really appreciate the anatomy of a fish until I moved to South Africa. My uncle had come to stay with us and he was a fan of fishing. There were several lakes near where we lived where you could fish, and he used to take my brother and cousin. On one occasion, he and my brother came back looking really sheepish. My brother said they had been caught fishing at a nearby lake when they weren't allowed to and were approached by a warden. They had escaped a fine by pretending they didn't know a word of English, and judging by my uncle's manner, they must have got a really bad telling-off because he didn't go fishing for weeks after that.

It was my uncle who taught us how to clean a fish: he would do so expertly as soon as he had caught the fish and then pack it into a cool-bag. After killing the fish, he would descale the skin with his knife and then proceed to take out the gills, stomach, intestines and heart. One time he gutted a fish in front of our dog, Guo Chung; he was barking so loudly we think he must have been traumatised by the experience, poor thing!

Despite the gore, Uncle would cook us all sorts of fishy dishes, whether grilled, steamed or fried. Twenty years on, he is now a vegetarian! Who would have thought he would put his fishing days behind him. When I ask him about those times, he says he regrets killing so many fish, but he also says that my aunt made him stop because their business kept failing and she believed he was killing all their *yu*, or fortune. He still has a glint in his eye that tells me a part of him misses it. After all, there is nothing more pleasurable and natural than being at one with nature and catching and preparing your own food.

It is the fruits of the sea rather than the lake that appear on the takeaway menu. Most takeaway dishes use prawns and sometimes scallops as the main ingredient, usually cooked in a sweet and sour, black bean or spicy Sichuan sauce. I have included some of my favourite takeaway flavours here but pairing them in a different way, so you will find Black Bean Mussels, for instance, Squid and King Prawns in Chilli Tomato Sauce with Courgettes, or XO Sauce and Pak Choi Squid, (see pages 122, 127 and 130). There are fish dishes too, such as Steamed Sea Bass in Spinach Sauce and Breaded Mackerel with Sichuan Pepper, Chilli and Salt (see pages 136 and 134) – a spicy, Eastern twist on that classic British takeaway, fish and chips.

Black bean mussels

Black beans are one of my all-time favourite ingredients. They're so versatile and work with all meats as well as seafood. This is a delicious dish, full of flavour and so quick. It's also great for dinner parties – just make sure you have a large enough wok!

PREP TIME: 15 minutes • **COOK IN:** 7 minutes • **SERVES:** 2–4 to share

500g (1lb 2oz) mussels

1 tbsp of groundnut oil

2 cloves of garlic, crushed and finely chopped

2.5cm (1in) piece of root ginger, peeled and sliced

2 red chillies, deseeded and finely chopped

1 tbsp of fermented salted black beans, rinsed and crushed

1 tbsp of Shaohsing rice wine or dry sherry

1 spring onion, sliced on the diagonal into 2.5cm (1in) pieces

FOR THE SAUCE

100ml (3½fl oz) vegetable stock

1 tbsp of light soy sauce

1 tbsp of dark soy sauce

1 tbsp of cornflour mixed with 1 tbsp of water

1. First scrub the mussels, removing any bits of 'beard' attached to the shells and discarding any that remain open when tapped against a hard surface.

2. Heat a wok over a high heat until it starts to smoke and then add the groundnut oil. Add the garlic, ginger, chillies and black beans and stir-fry for a few seconds. Tip in the mussels and stir-fry for a few seconds more. As the shells start to open up, season with the rice wine or dry sherry.

3. Pour in the ingredients for the sauce, then bring to the boil and cook for 5 minutes or until the sauce has reduced and thickened and all the shells have opened. (Discard any that remain unopened.) Stir in the spring onions, then transfer to a large bowl and serve immediately.

Nutty prawn, asparagus and cashew nut stir-fry

The crunchy roasted cashew nuts make this a very moreish dish. It is perfect served with some boiled rice and great as a midweek supper.

PREP TIME: 5 minutes • **COOK IN:** 7 minutes • **SERVES:** 2

200g (7oz) tender asparagus spears, woody ends snapped off, then cut into thirds

1 tbsp of groundnut oil

2 cloves of garlic, crushed and finely chopped

2.5cm (1in) piece of root ginger, peeled and grated

150g (5oz) cooked shelled and deveined tiger prawns

1 tbsp of Shaohsing rice wine or dry sherry

1 tbsp of light soy sauce

1 tsp of clear rice vinegar or cider vinegar

Handful of roasted salted cashew nuts

1 tsp of cornflour mixed with 1 tbsp of water

1 tbsp of toasted sesame oil

1. Bring a small saucepan of water to the boil, add the asparagus pieces and blanch for 2 minutes, then drain and refresh under cold running water to stop them from cooking further. Put on a plate and set aside.

2. Heat a wok over a high heat until it starts to smoke and then add the groundnut oil. Add the garlic and ginger and stir-fry a few seconds, then tip in the blanched asparagus pieces. Stir-fry for 2 minutes and then add the prawns and stir-fry for another minute.

3. Add the rice wine or dry sherry, followed by the soy sauce, vinegar and cashew nuts. Add the cornflour paste to thicken the sauce, stir in the toasted sesame oil and serve immediately.

Spicy sweet king prawns

This is a take on my mum's ketchup prawns, which are really delicious. I have simply added chilli to give it a kick. Sweet, spicy and tangy, this dish is delicious with boiled rice and some steamed vegetables.

PREP TIME: 10 minutes • **COOK IN:** 5 minutes • **SERVES:** 2–4 to share

1 tbsp of groundnut oil

2.5cm (1in) piece of root ginger, peeled and sliced

300g (11oz) raw king prawns in the shell, deveined (see the tip below)

1 tbsp of Shaohsing rice wine or dry sherry

2 tbsps of tomato ketchup

2 tbsps of chilli sauce

1 spring onion, sliced, to garnish

1. Heat a wok over a high heat until it starts to smoke and then add the groundnut oil. Add the ginger and fry for 1 second, then tip in the prawns straight away and stir-fry for 1 minute.

2. As the prawns start to turn pink, add the rice wine or dry sherry and cook for 2 minutes, then season with the ketchup and chilli sauce. Toss well in the wok, then garnish with the sliced spring onion and serve immediately.

> **CHING'S TIP**
> To devein the prawns, simply run a sharp knife along the back of each prawn and remove the vein with the tip of the knife. My grandmother would use a toothpick – pierce the skin between the head and body and pull the toothpick along the length, pulling the vein out with it. This ensures that the flesh and shell stay intact; cooking the prawns with the shell on seals in the flavour and juices.

Healthy sweet and sour king prawn stir-fry

This is such a simple sweet and sour dish, made with delicious king prawns and a quick and easy sauce – a stir-fry that's ready in minutes.

PREP TIME: 10 minutes • **COOK IN:** 7 minutes • **SERVES:** 2

50g (2oz) tinned pineapple chunks

200ml (7fl oz) pineapple juice

2 tbsps of groundnut oil

6 large raw shelled and deveined king prawns, tails left on

1 tbsp of peeled and grated root ginger

1 red chilli, deseeded and finely chopped

½ onion, cut into chunks

Small handful of red and yellow pepper chunks

Small handful of bean sprouts

Salt and ground white pepper

Juice of 1 small lime

1 tsp of runny honey

1 spring onion, finely sliced, to garnish

1. Place the pineapple chunks and juice in a blender and whiz to a purée, then remove from the blender and set aside.

2. Heat a wok over a high heat until it starts to smoke and then add half the groundnut oil. Add the prawns and stir-fry for 2–3 minutes or until they turn pink, then set aside.

3. Heat the remaining groundnut oil in the wok and stir-fry the ginger and chilli for a few seconds, then add the onion and stir-fry for 1 minute or until softened.

4. Add the pineapple purée and let the sauce reduce for 1 minute, then stir in the pepper chunks and bean sprouts and cook for another minute.

5. Season to taste with salt and pepper and add the lime juice and honey, then tip in the cooked prawns and stir together. Check the seasoning, adding more if necessary, and sprinkle with the spring onion. Serve immediately with boiled jasmine rice.

King prawns in chilli tomato sauce with courgettes

First you make the chilli tomato paste and then add king prawns for a tasty, moreish dish. If you fancy a change from boiled rice, add some cooked egg noodles at the end to turn this into a spicy chow mein.

PREP TIME: 10 minutes • **COOK IN:** 5 minutes • **SERVES:** 2

1 tbsp of groundnut oil

1 red chilli, deseeded and finely chopped

1 courgette, grated

350g (12oz) large raw shelled and deveined king prawns

1 tbsp of Shaohsing rice wine or dry sherry

1 tbsp of light soy sauce or to taste

Small handful of chopped coriander

FOR THE TOMATO PASTE

1 onion, diced

1 red chilli, deseeded and roughly chopped

2 small ripe tomatoes, roughly chopped

2 tbsps of tomato ketchup

1 tbsp of soft light brown sugar

1 tbsp of light soy sauce

1. Put all the ingredients for the tomato paste into a blender and whiz together. Remove from the blender and set aside.

2. Heat a wok over a high heat until it starts to smoke and then add the groundnut oil. Add the red chilli and fry for a few seconds, then add the courgette and stir-fry for 1 minute.

3. Tip in the prawns and cook for 30 seconds, adding the rice wine or dry sherry as the prawns start to turn pink. Add the tomato paste, then bring to the boil and cook for 2 minutes.

4. Season further to taste with the soy sauce, then garnish with the chopped coriander and serve immediately.

Steamed giant Madagascar prawns with yellow bean sauce and garlic spinach

This dish is perfect for an intimate meal for two. Delicious as well as healthy, it's not exactly takeaway fare, but an adapted version of this recipe – such as stir-fried prawns in yellow bean sauce – would certainly work well as a takeaway dish!

PREP TIME: 10 minutes • **COOK IN:** 10 minutes • **SERVES:** 2

2 giant Madagascar prawns in the shells deveined (see the tip on page 124)

2.5cm (1in) piece of root ginger, peeled and sliced into matchsticks

1 tbsp Shaohsing rice wine or dry sherry

1 red chilli, deseeded and finely chopped, or 1 spring onion, finely chopped, to garnish (optional)

FOR THE SAUCE

1 tbsp of groundnut oil

2 cloves of garlic, crushed

2 tbsps of yellow bean sauce

50ml (2fl oz) vegetable stock

1 tsp of light soy sauce

FOR THE GARLIC SPINACH

1 tbsp of groundnut oil

1 clove of garlic, crushed and finely chopped

2 large handfuls of baby spinach leaves

1 pinch of sea salt

1. Place the prawns on a heatproof plate that will fit inside a large bamboo steamer. Scatter the ginger on top and drizzle with the rice wine or dry sherry. Place the steamer over a wok or saucepan filled with boiling water (making sure the bottom of the steamer does not touch the water). Put the lid on and steam the prawns on a high heat for 8 minutes.

2. Meanwhile, for the sauce, heat a small wok over a high heat until it starts to smoke and then add the groundnut oil. Add the garlic and stir for a few seconds, then add the yellow bean sauce, stock and soy sauce, and stir to combine. Bring to the boil, then reduce the heat to very low to keep warm.

3. Heat another small wok or saucepan over a medium heat and add the groundnut oil. Add the garlic and stir for a few seconds, then add the spinach and toss in the garlic oil until wilted. Season with the salt and set aside.

4. To serve, remove the prawns from the steamer and place one on each plate. Keeping the head and tail on, peel away just one side of the shell of each prawn to expose the meat, then drizzle over 2 tbsps of the sauce. Decorate with the garlic from the sauce. Spoon a mound of spinach on to the plate, garnish with the chopped red chilli or spring onion and serve immediately.

XO sauce and pak choy squid

XO sauce is the crème de la crème of Cantonese sauces. It is made from chopped dried seafood, such as shrimps and scallops, and dried fish, cooked with garlic, onions and chilli and preserved in oil. The name XO comes from 'Extra-Old', referring to extra-old cognac, a symbol of luxury and quality; hence the term 'XO' indicates something that is the ultimate in quality.

PREP TIME: 10 minutes • **COOK IN:** 5 minutes • **SERVES:** 2–4 to share

1 tbsp of groundnut oil

2 dried red chillies

1 tbsp of peeled and grated root ginger

2 large pak choy cut into strips

500g (1lb 2oz) squid, cleaned, chopped into 5cm (2in) pieces and scored criss-cross fashion on the underside of the skin

1 tbsp of Shaohsing rice wine or dry sherry

2 tbsps of XO sauce

1 tbsp of light soy sauce

1. Heat a wok over a high heat until it starts to smoke and then add the groundnut oil. Add the ginger and chilles and fry for 1 second. Tip in the pak choy and stir-fry for another few seconds, then add the squid and stir-fry for 2 minutes.

2. As the squid starts to turn opaque and curl up, add the rice wine or dry sherry. Pour in the XO sauce and stir all the ingredients together. Season with the soy sauce and serve immediately with jasmine or brown rice.

Ginger and mushroom wined clams

This dish is warming, light and earthy in flavour. You could always turn it into a nourishing broth by adding more vegetable stock and have it with some slices of buttered soda bread for a light supper, which would give you the best of East and West.

PREP TIME: 15 minutes • **COOK IN:** 7 minutes • **SERVES:** 2

300g (11oz) clams
1 tbsp of groundnut oil
2.5cm (1in) piece of root ginger, peeled and sliced into matchsticks
2 tbsps of dried shrimps, soaked in hot water for 20 minutes, then drained (optional)
3 dried Chinese mushrooms, soaked in hot water for 20 minutes, then drained and sliced, or 3 shiitake mushrooms, sliced
4 tbsps of Shaohsing rice wine or dry sherry
100ml (3½fl oz) vegetable stock
Salt and ground white pepper
1 tbsp of cornflour mixed with 1 tbsp of water
Large handful of coriander

1. First scrub the clams, removing any debris from the shells and discarding any that remain open when tapped against a hard surface.

2. Heat a wok over a high heat until it starts to smoke and then add the groundnut oil. Add the ginger, dried shrimps (if using) and mushrooms and stir-fry for a few seconds. Tip in the clams and stir-fry for 1 minute.

3. As the shells start to open up, add the rice wine or dry sherry. Pour in the stock and cook for 3–4 minutes or until all the shells have opened. Discard any that remain closed.

4. Season to taste with salt and pepper and thicken the cooking liquid with the cornflour paste. Toss in the coriander and let it wilt slightly, then remove from the heat, transfer to a large dish and serve immediately.

Breaded mackerel with Sichuan pepper, chilli and salt

This is my way of incorporating oily fish into my diet. Of course you can also wok-fry mackerel with garlic, ginger, light soy, toasted sesame oil, rice wine and a pinch of sugar, and serve with boiled rice and steamed vegetables, but I also love this naughty 'yang' way of cooking it.

PREP TIME: 10 minutes • **COOK IN:** 10 minutes • **SERVES:** 2

300g (11oz) mackerel fillets, skin on

4 tbsps of plain flour

2 eggs, beaten

8 tbsps of panko breadcrumbs

1 tbsp of Sichuan peppercorns, toasted and ground (see the tip on page 49)

1 tbsp of dried chilli flakes

½ tsp of sea salt

500ml (18fl oz) groundnut oil

1. Rinse the mackerel fillets in cold running water and pat dry on kitchen paper. Cut the fillets into 4cm (1½in) slices and set aside. Place the flour, beaten eggs and breadcrumbs in three separate bowls.

2. In another small bowl, mix the ground Sichuan peppercorns with the chilli flakes and sea salt and set to one side.

3. Place a wok over a high heat, then pour in the groundnut oil and heat until 180°C (350°F) or until a cube of bread dropped in turns golden brown in 15 seconds and floats to the surface.

4. Place a piece of the fish in the flour (shaking off any excess flour), then dip into the egg and coat in the breadcrumbs. Repeat with all the pieces of fish and place in a bowl, then carefully lower one batch into the hot oil using a slotted spoon. When the batter turns golden brown, lift out the fish and drain any excess oil on a plate lined with kitchen paper and keep warm. Continue until all the fish has been cooked.

5. Sprinkle the spice mixture over the fish, toss together well and serve immediately with chunky chips or, for a healthier alternative, shredded lettuce leaves, thin carrot strips and sliced fresh chillies.

Steamed sea bass with ginger and mushrooms

In China, fish are mostly cooked whole, including the head, because the cheek (just below the eyes) is considered the best part. The eyes and lips are a delicacy too. Keeping the fish whole during cooking also symbolises completeness and unity, which is important for Chinese New Year and other auspicious events in the Chinese calendar. The relatively large quantity of rice wine provides a fragrant bittersweet flavour and works wonderfully well with the aromatic mushrooms, hot ginger, tangy spring onions and of course the sweet flesh of the fish.

PREP TIME: 10 minutes • **COOK IN:** 11 minutes • **SERVES:** 2–4 to share

1 whole sea bass (about 400g/14oz), gutted and descaled

Salt and ground white pepper

5cm (2in) piece of root ginger, peeled and sliced

4 dried Chinese mushrooms, soaked in hot water for 20 minutes, then drained, stalks removed and sliced, or 4 shiitake mushrooms, sliced

4 tbsps of Shaohsing rice wine or dry sherry

50g (2oz) oyster mushrooms

2 spring onions, sliced lengthways into 7cm (2¾in) lengths

1. Place the fish on a heatproof plate that will fit inside a bamboo steamer. Cut a few slits in the skin on both sides, then season with salt and pepper. Place some slices of ginger and Chinese or shiitake mushroom into the slits and inside the fish.

2. Sprinkle over the rice wine or dry sherry, then place the plate in the steamer and close the lid. Set the steamer over a wok or saucepan filled with boiling water (making sure the bottom of the steamer doesn't touch the water) and steam over a high heat for 8–9 minutes or until the fish is cooked and the flesh flakes easily to the point of a knife.

3. Lay the oyster mushrooms and spring onions on top of the fish and steam for a further 2 minutes. Remove the steamer from the wok or pan, keeping the lid closed until ready to serve. Serve with jasmine rice and stir-fried vegetables.

> **ALSO TRY**
> You may use any white-fleshed fish for this dish and you could steam fillets rather than the whole fish, if you preferred.

Steamed sea bass in spinach sauce

This is a delicious way to serve steamed sea bass – in a spinach and garlic sauce. It's easy to make, nutritious and fuss-free. The hardest part is getting your hands on the freshest-possible fish.

PREP TIME: 10 minutes • **COOK IN:** 10 minutes • **SERVES:** 2

2 wild sea bass fillets
Sea salt and ground white pepper
1 tbsp of Shaohsing rice wine or dry sherry
1 tbsp of peeled and grated root ginger
1 tbsp of light soy sauce or to taste
1 tbsp of cornflour mixed with 1 tbsp of water

FOR THE SAUCE
1 tbsp of groundnut oil
3 cloves of garlic, crushed
1 red chilli, deseeded and finely chopped
Large bunch of coriander
Large handful of spinach leaves
100ml (3½fl oz) cold vegetable stock

1. Place the sea bass fillets on a heatproof plate that will fit inside a bamboo steamer. Season the fish with salt and pepper, drizzle over the rice wine or dry sherry and rub the grated ginger over the flesh of the fish.

2. Put the plate inside the steamer and cover with the lid. Set the steamer over a wok or saucepan filled with boiling water (making sure the bottom of the steamer does not touch the water). Steam for 10 minutes on a high heat or until the flesh of the fish flakes easily to the point of a knife. Keep the fish warm in the steamer until ready to serve.

3. Meanwhile, place all the ingredients for the sauce in a blender and blitz together, then set aside.

4. Heat a small wok or saucepan over a high heat and pour in the sauce, then season to taste with the soy sauce. Bring the sauce to a simmer, add the cornflour paste and stir until thickened, then remove from the heat. Transfer the sea bass fillets to individual plates, pour over the sauce and serve with Special Mixed Vegetables (see page 155) and jasmine rice.

> **ALSO TRY**
> This recipe can be adapted for any white-fleshed fish, including pollack or haddock.

Steamed plaice with black beans

Black bean sauce is a popular ingredient in so many takeaway dishes. There is no need to buy it, however, because you can just as easily use the whole beans, and they taste so much better. I love pairing the beans with fish, as in this recipe inspired by a Cantonese dish served in Chinese restaurants. I've simply substituted plaice for the sea bass or pomfret that is usually incorporated in this dish.

PREP TIME: 5 minutes • **COOK IN:** 10 minutes • **SERVES:** 2 to share

1 whole plaice (about 600g/1lb 5oz), gutted and descaled

2.5cm (1in) piece of root ginger, peeled and sliced into matchsticks

1 tbsp of Shaohsing rice wine or dry sherry

1 tbsp of light soy sauce

1 tbsp of fermented salted black beans, rinsed and lightly crushed

2 spring onions, sliced lengthways

1. Score the sides of the plaice, then stuff the ginger slices into the slits as well as the body of the fish.

2. Place the fish on a heatproof plate that will fit inside a large bamboo steamer and drizzle the rice wine or dry sherry over the fish, followed by the soy sauce. Sprinkle over the black beans, then drape the spring onions over the fish and place the lid on the steamer.

3. Place the steamer over a wok or saucepan filled with boiling water (making sure the bottom of the steamer does not touch the water) and steam the plaice over a high heat for 10 minutes or until the flesh of the fish has turned opaque and flakes easily when poked with a chopstick or knife.

4. Remove from the steamer and serve with Buddha's Stir-fried Mixed Vegetables or Pak choy with Carrot and Garlic (see pages 156 and 144) and some boiled rice.

Vegetarian

When I was 13, I turned vegetarian for almost a year, inspired by a trip to Taiwan. It was the summer holidays and my brother and I had gone back to visit my mum. She and my father had decided to set up an import–export business. She would be based in Taipei and my father would stay in London to look after us. It wasn't ideal, but my parents wanted my brother and me to have the best education possible and it seemed the only way forward after several failed business attempts following our move to London in 1989 and recession hitting in 1990.

We were happy to see Mum and spent some time with her in Taipei as well as visiting my grandparents and all the relatives in Kaohsiung, in the south. After visiting our relatives, my mum suggested we go to the Tzu-Chi Foundation based in the small village of Hua Lien, on the eastern coast of Taiwan. The Tzu-Chi abode is a special place, set up by a Buddhist nun, the venerable Master Cheng-Yen, an incredible woman with a big heart. Thousands of volunteers sign up each year to give their time to help with the organisation's many charitable causes.

The abode is a beautiful, serene place. Two nuns with beaming, welcoming smiles greeted us. They led us to a courtyard with a temple behind it and we bowed to show our respect. The whole place was very quiet, so quiet you could hear the birds chirping. One of the nuns led us to a small building where there was a strong smell of incense. She said the Master Cheng-Yen would be able to see us in a few minutes. We sat on small round wooden stools and sipped oolong tea. We were all very excited and waited with nervous anticipation. Master Cheng-Yen came into the room and was introduced by another nun. She was a small fragile woman with bright eyes and a warm smile. I don't know what happened but I was overcome with emotion and the tears flowed naturally; I was unable to stop them. The master patted me on the head and told me to stop crying. She asked me whether I could write Chinese. I replied that I wasn't very good at it and she told me to try harder and never to forget where I was from. My mum's friend, who was accompanying us, said that she also cried the first time she saw the master and she told me it was a sign of 'coming home'.

At 12 noon a bell rang to signal that it was time for lunch. We were shown to the main dining room where we sat down on stools at simple round wooden tables. The dishes were already laid out, with the smell of rice wafting through the air. There must have been over a hundred people in that dining room, but there wasn't a sound. We said a blessing and then we had to take a grain of rice first from the eastern part of the bowl, then the western part and then the middle, to show our appreciation of the dish. Then we helped ourselves to an array of delicacies, all of which were vegetarian. There were stir-fried vegetables, braised bean curd and stir-fried wheat gluten and dofu – all simply cooked but full of flavour. When the meal was over, we poured a small amount of hot water into our bowls and, using a piece of vegetable, 'washed' the dish and then drank the liquid – a ritual called *xi-fu* ('preserving fortune'), acknowledging what a blessing it is to have food and that none should be wasted, for wasted food is a sign of wasted fortune. At the end of the meal, not one bowl had a speck of food left in it. It was a life-changing experience.

The nuns grew their own vegetables, made candles and sewed socks, which they sold to make a living. The master's wise Buddhist teachings and quotes were published in books and sold to raise money to support the place. The whole community was self-sufficient and any profits were donated to charity. That afternoon, I helped the nuns pick vegetables and wash and prepare them for dinner, listened to their stories and learned more about Buddhism. I was so moved by the whole experience that when we left I told my mum I was going to be a vegetarian, and I was for almost a year.

Sad to say that the dish that broke me was the hot bacon sandwiches served at break-time at school! But I have never forgotten what I learned at Tzu-Chi: following the Buddhists' etiquette at table, inspired by their compassion for all living beings, I always say a blessing of thanks for the animals that have sacrificed their lives.

Good Buddhists themselves, my grandparents always treasured the animals they kept on their farm. They ate chicken only if it was too old to lay eggs, while pigs were bred to sell and eaten only on special occasions. On the 15th of the lunar calendar every month, we ate only vegetables, to show our compassion for animals. I still try to do this every month, and I have my family to thank for making me a more mindful and considerate cook.

Vegetarian dishes are usually quite limited on a standard takeaway menu. If I were running my own takeaway or diner, I'd serve far more and I've tried to expand the range here, offering a variety of recipes that would work both as side dishes or as a meal in their own right.

Bean sprout and spring onion stir-fry

This is a simple, tasty and economical dish that is very quick to make. To a Chinese cook, bean sprouts are the equivalent of potatoes to a Western cook. The most commonly used vegetable in Chinese cuisine, they add texture and crunch to a huge range of dishes, from stir-fries and soups to salads.

PREP TIME: 5 minutes • **COOK IN:** 3 minutes • **SERVES:** 2–4 to share

1 tbsp of groundnut oil
2.5cm (1in) piece of root ginger, peeled and sliced
Handful of bean sprouts
1 tbsp of light soy sauce
1 spring onion, finely sliced

1. Heat a wok over a high heat until it starts to smoke. Add the groundnut oil and ginger and fry for a few seconds. Tip in the bean sprouts and toss, then add a small dash of water to create some steam and cook for 1 minute or until the bean sprouts start to wilt. Season with the soy sauce, stir in the spring onion and serve immediately.

Pak choy with carrot and garlic

Pak choy (or 'bok choy') is a leafy vegetable much used in Chinese cooking, especially soups and stir-fries. I love both the green- and white-stemmed varieties.

PREP TIME: 5 minutes • **COOK IN:** 4 minutes • **SERVES:** 2–4 to share

1 tbsp of groundnut oil
1 clove of garlic, crushed and finely chopped
1 small carrot, thinly sliced on the diagonal
200g (7oz) baby pak choy, leaves separated (see the tip below)
2 pinches of coarse sea salt

1. Heat a wok over a high heat until it starts to smoke, then add the groundnut oil and the garlic and cook for a few seconds. Add the carrot slices and stir-fry for 2 minutes. Tip in the pak choy leaves and toss. Add a small dash of water and cook for 1 minute. Sprinkle over the sea salt and serve immediately.

> **CHING'S TIP**
> If you are using the larger, green-stemmed pak choy, then separate the leaves from the stalks, slice the stalks and stir-fry with the carrot for 2 minutes before adding the leaves and stir-frying for 1 further minute.

Lotus root salad

Lotus flowers have been grown in China for thousands of years. Several parts of the plant are edible, including the stem, also known as the root, which can be bought from Chinese supermarkets, sold fresh in vacuum packs. The roots are knobbly in appearance, and when you slice through one crossways, you can see a series of holes, rather like the 'rose' of a watering can. Look out for firm short roots without any markings. You can eat lotus roots raw, although I prefer to blanch mine in boiling water for a few minutes to get rid of any unwanted bacteria, since these grow buried in muddy waters. Delightfully crunchy and sweet, they resemble water chestnuts in texture, with a delicate flavour like bamboo shoots.

PREP TIME: 10 minutes, plus 20 minutes for chilling
COOK IN: 2 minutes • **SERVES:** 2–4 to share

200g (7oz) fresh lotus roots
1 red chilli, deseeded and finely chopped
Small handful of coriander, finely chopped, to garnish

FOR THE DRESSING
1 tbsp of toasted sesame oil
1 tbsp of clear rice vinegar or cider vinegar
1 tbsp of light soy sauce
Pinch of salt
Pinch of caster sugar

1. To prepare the lotus roots, first cut through the joints between the segments, then peel the skin and place in a saucepan of boiling water to blanch for 2 minutes. Rinse in cold water to refresh, then slice finely, using a mandolin if possible.

2. Mix together the ingredients for the dressing in a large bowl, then add the sliced lotus roots and toss in the dressing to coat. Cover with cling film and chill for 20 minutes in the fridge. Serve garnished with the chopped coriander.

Sweet roasted vegetables

Sweet potatoes are thought to have originated in tropical South America and then made their way to Europe. Chinese explorers are believed to have brought these to Asia in the mid-15th century. They were certainly common enough when we were growing up in Taiwan. We used to wrap them in newspaper and 'kong' them – that is, bury them in a hole in the ground filled with twigs and stones and allow them to slow-cook for a few hours until tender. It was the most delicious thing! I also love them roasted Western-style with other sweet vegetables and Chinese spices. It makes a great accompaniment to a Chinese roast.

PREP TIME: 20 minutes • **COOK IN:** 20 minutes • **SERVES:** 2–4 to share

2 red peppers, deseeded and chopped into 5cm (2in) pieces

2 red onions, cut into wedges

2 sweet potatoes (unpeeled), sliced into wedges

2 parsnips (unpeeled), sliced into wedges

4 tbsps of groundnut oil or olive oil

2 tsps of runny honey

FOR THE SPICE MIX

1 tsp of sea salt

1 tsp of black peppercorns

1 tbsp of soft light brown sugar

1 tbsp of Chinese five-spice powder

1 small piece of cassia bark or cinnamon stick

2 cloves

1 star anise

1. Preheat the oven to 180°C (350°F), gas mark 4.

2. Put all the spices in a spice grinder, or use a pestle and mortar, and grind them into a fine powder.

3. Place all the prepared vegetables in a roasting tin and toss together. Sprinkle the spice mix over the vegetables and drizzle over the groundnut oil or olive oil and the honey. Toss together in the tin and then roast in the oven for 20 minutes or until golden.

Yellow bean sesame spinach

This makes a simple but elegant accompaniment to any meat or fish dish, or served with stir-fried vegetables for a vegetarian option. It is very quick to make and full of flavour. If you can, try and buy leafier savoy or semi-savoy spinach, with larger leaves, as opposed to baby spinach.

PREP TIME: 10 minutes • **COOK IN:** 5 minutes • **SERVES:** 2–4 to share

450g (1lb) fresh young spinach

4 tsps of white sesame seeds, toasted (see the tip on page 44)

FOR THE SAUCE

1 tbsp of groundnut oil

1 tsp of peeled and grated root ginger

1 tsp of yellow bean sauce

1 tbsp of light soy sauce

50ml (2fl oz) cold vegetable stock

1 tsp of cornflour mixed with 1 tbsp water

1. Bring a large saucepan of water to the boil. Add the spinach leaves and blanch for 20 seconds, then remove and drain well in a colander. Rinse the wilted leaves under cold running water, then squeeze out the excess water and set to one side.

2. Heat a wok over a high heat until it starts to smoke, then add all the ingredients for the sauce and bring to the boil. Allow the sauce to thicken and then remove from the heat.

3. Form the drained spinach into a log shape, about 10cm (4in) long, then slice it into quarters. Stand the log shapes on a serving plate, top with the toasted sesame seeds and drizzle the sauce around the plate using a spoon. Serve immediately.

Dou miao with enoki mushrooms

Dou miao are the immature shoots of the sugar snap pea or snow pea and are prized for their super-tender, sweet and delicious stems. They can be found in Chinese supermarkets, although they are more expensive than other leafy greens used in Chinese cuisine. Usually they are added to soups at the last minute, or cooked in a simple stir-fry with stock and some garlic and ginger. I love to serve them stir-fried with enoki mushrooms. These have a very long, thin stem with a tiny golden head (hence their other name, golden needle mushrooms) and in the wild can be found growing on the Chinese hackberry tree. They can be eaten raw or added to stir-fries at the end of cooking to retain their sweet and delicate flavour. This is an elegant recipe, great as an accompaniment for the main dish at a dinner party.

PREP TIME: 5 minutes • **COOK IN:** 3 minutes • **SERVES:** 2–4 to share

1 tbsp of groundnut oil
Few pinches of coarse sea salt
2 cloves of garlic, crushed and finely chopped
200g (7oz) *dou miao* shoots
100g (3½oz) enoki mushrooms
100ml (3½fl oz) vegetable stock
Pinch of ground white pepper

1. Heat a wok over a high heat until it starts to smoke and then add the groundnut oil. Add the sea salt followed by the garlic and then add the *dou miao* and stir-fry together for 2 minutes or until the leaves wilt.

2. Break in the enoki mushrooms and toss all the ingredients together. Pour in the vegetable stock, season with the ground white pepper and serve immediately.

Oriental mushrooms with black bean sauce

In this dish, the mushrooms act like a sponge to soak up all the delicious flavours of the black bean sauce. You can buy ready-made black bean sauce, but there is nothing more rewarding than making your own: it's easy and quick, and packs a far more powerful flavour!

PREP TIME: 10 minutes • **COOK IN:** 5 minutes • **SERVES:** 2–4 to share

1 tbsp of groundnut oil

2 cloves of garlic, crushed and finely chopped

1 tbsp peeled and grated ginger root

1 red chilli, deseeded and finely chopped

1 tbsp of fermented salted black beans, rinsed and crushed

350g (12oz) mixed oriental mushrooms (such as shimeji, oyster and shiitake), sliced

1 tbsp of Shaohsing rice wine or dry sherry

1 spring onion, finely chopped

FOR THE SAUCE

150ml (5fl oz) cold vegetable stock

1–2 tbsps of light soy sauce

1 tbsp of cornflour mixed with 1 tbsp water

1. Heat a wok over a high heat until it starts to smoke and then add the groundnut oil. Add the garlic, ginger, chilli and crushed black beans and stir-fry for a few seconds. Toss in the mushrooms and stir together, then add the rice wine or dry sherry and stir for a few seconds.

2. Add the ingredients for the sauce and bring to the boil. As the sauce thickens, stir in the spring onion, then transfer to a serving dish and serve immediately with jasmine rice.

Light choy sum with oyster sauce

Choy sum ('vegetable heart' in Cantonese) is a popular leafy vegetable that is also known as flowering cabbage because of the yellow flower the plant produces. The leaves and stem are both tender when cooked and provide a sweet, mild flavour. It can be blanched and added to soups, as well as stir-fried or steamed.

PREP TIME: 5 minutes • **COOK IN:** 3 minutes • **SERVES:** 2–4 to share

Large bunch of choy sum

2 tbsps of vegetarian oyster sauce

1. Bring a large saucepan of water to the boil, then add the choy sum and blanch for 2–3 minutes. Drain in a colander and transfer to a serving plate, then drizzle over the oyster sauce (the latent heat from the cooked leaves will heat up the sauce) and serve immediately.

Pickled salad

I love pickled Chinese vegetables, especially as an appetiser, as they help to 'wake' the tastebuds. This is a simple dish that works well as an accompaniment to a spicy main dish, giving cooling relief. It is also delicious as a topping on *gua bao* (see page 171).

PREP TIME: 10 minutes, plus 20 minutes for chilling • **SERVES:** 2–4 to share

½ cucumber (unpeeled), de-seeded and very finely sliced

1 carrot, finely sliced on the diagonal

6 small radishes, finely sliced

1 tbsp of mirin

3 tbsps of clear rice vinegar or cider vinegar

1 tsp of caster sugar

¼ tsp of coarse sea salt

1. Add all the ingredients to a large bowl, then toss together, cover with cling film and chill in the fridge for 20 minutes before serving.

Fish-fragrant aubergine with dofu

This is an adaptation of one of my favourite Sichuan dishes. It doesn't actually contain any fish but is called 'fish-fragrant' or *yu xiang* because of the stock it is cooked in. (See also Fish-fragrant Aubergine with Pork on page 115.) You can use standard Western aubergines for this dish, but if you can, try to get hold of the long Asian variety, which are sweeter and more tender. The traditional way of cooking the aubergine is to deep-fry it in oil and then stir-fry with the remaining ingredients, but this version is healthier and works just as well in my opinion.

PREP TIME: 10 minutes • **COOK IN:** 8 minutes • **SERVES:** 2–4 to share

2 tbsps of groundnut oil

1 aubergine, sliced into batons

2 cloves of garlic, crushed and finely chopped

2.5cm (1in) piece of root ginger, peeled and grated

1 red chilli, deseeded and finely chopped

1 tbsp of chilli bean sauce

200g (7oz) fresh firm dofu, drained and cut into 1.5cm (⅝in) cubes

1 spring onion, finely sliced

FOR THE SAUCE

100ml (3½fl oz) cold vegetable stock

1 tbsp of light soy sauce

1 tbsp of Chinkiang black rice vinegar or balsamic vinegar

1 tbsp of cornflour mixed with 1 tbsp of water

1. Heat a wok over a high heat until it starts to smoke and then add half the groundnut oil. Add the aubergine and stir-fry until browned, then cook, still stirring, for 5 minutes or until softened. During this process, keep adding small drops of water to create a little steam to help soften the aubergine as it cooks. Transfer to a plate and set aside.

2. Place the wok back over a high heat and add the remaining groundnut oil. Add the garlic, ginger, chilli and chilli bean sauce and cook together for a few seconds. Add the cooked aubergine, followed by all the ingredients for the sauce, then tip in the dofu and bring to the boil.

3. Cook until the sauce has thickened and then stir in spring onion. Remove from the heat and serve immediately with jasmine rice.

> **ALSO TRY**
> I like using fresh firm dofu in this dish, as it soaks up the flavours and adds protein, but if you are not a fan of dofu, you could substitute with shiitake mushrooms or chestnut mushrooms instead.

Special mixed vegetables

I rarely buy ready-prepared vegetables, but there is a place for them. I recently stumbled across a packet of assorted baby sweetcorn, mini broccoli florets, peas and grated carrots and I was most impressed with the quality and freshness. This sort of selection comes in very handy as an addition to quick-fried rice. It also makes a great accompaniment to other dishes. Fast, easy, delicious and nutritious, it could be served as an alternative to rice as part of a carb-free meal.

PREP TIME: 5 minutes • **COOK IN:** 4 minutes • **SERVES:** 2–4 to share

1 tbsp of groundnut oil

1 tbsp of peeled and finely grated root ginger

300g (11oz) ready-prepared mixed vegetables (such as baby sweetcorn, broccoli florets, peas and grated carrots)

1 tbsp of light soy sauce

1 tbsp of toasted sesame oil

Pinch of ground white pepper

1. Heat a wok over a high heat until it starts to smoke and then add the groundnut oil. Add the grated ginger and stir for a few seconds, then tip in the mixed vegetables and cook for 2 minutes, stirring constantly. Add a small dash of water to create some steam and help soften the vegetables, then season with the soy sauce, toasted sesame oil and white pepper and serve immediately.

ALSO TRY
For a more substantial vegetarian meal, you could add pieces of smoked marinated deep-fried dofu.

Buddha's stir-fried mixed vegetables

There are many variations on this classic dish, familiarly known as 'Buddha's delight', and traditionally it would also contain such ingredients as dried lily bulbs and straw mushrooms. This is my take on the dish. You can buy the wood ear mushrooms in a Chinese supermarket; if you can't find them, you can omit them, but they are worth seeking out because they are so versatile. They can be used in salads, soups, stir-fries, spring rolls, stews and dumplings. They are mostly available dried and will need pre-soaking in warm water before using. As they rehydrate, they double in size and can then be sliced before adding to whatever dish you're making. They have a bland taste but provide a great crunchy texture and this recipe wouldn't be the same without them.

PREP TIME: 15 minutes • **COOK IN:** 5 minutes • **SERVES:** 2–4 to share

1 tbsp of groundnut oil

1 tbsp of peeled and grated root ginger

1 carrot, cut into matchsticks

Small handful of dried Chinese wood ear mushrooms, soaked in hot water for 20 minutes, drained and sliced

Small handful of baby sweetcorn, sliced lengthways

1 x 225g tin of bamboo shoots, drained and cut into matchsticks

Small handful of bean sprouts

2 spring onions, finely sliced

FOR THE SAUCE

100ml (3½fl oz) cold vegetable stock

1 tbsp of light soy sauce

1 tbsp of vegetarian oyster sauce

1 tsp of toasted sesame oil

1 tbsp of cornflour

1. Heat a wok over a high heat until it starts to smoke and then add the groundnut oil. Add the grated ginger and stir-fry for a few seconds. Tip in the carrot, mushrooms, baby sweetcorn and bamboo shoots and stir-fry for 2 minutes.

2. Meanwhile, mix all the sauce ingredients together in a small bowl.

3. Add the sauce to the wok and bring to the boil. When the sauce has thickened, reduce the heat, then add the bean sprouts and spring onions and cook for 1 minute. Transfer to a serving plate and serve with jasmine rice.

Mock duck and tenderstem broccoli stir-fry

A Chinese menu has much to offer a vegetarian thanks to the abundance of assorted ingredients made predominantly from soya and wheat gluten and including mock pork, mock duck, mock chicken and even mock tuna and swordfish! When added to dishes that would normally contain meat, these substitutes can easily fool you, as they taste like the real thing. I recently had a Kung Po 'chicken' dish, only to be told it wasn't made with chicken. You may be able to find some tinned varieties in a Chinese supermarket. If you can't, then use vegetarian sausages, sliced up, instead.

PREP TIME: 15 minutes • **COOK IN:** 5 minutes • **SERVES:** 2–4 to share

2 tbsps of groundnut oil

1 clove of garlic, crushed and finely chopped

1 tbsp of peeled and grated root ginger

1 red chilli, deseeded and finely chopped

4 shiitake mushrooms, sliced

1 x 190g tin of mock duck, rinsed, drained and sliced

100g (3½oz) tenderstem broccoli, sliced on the diagonal

100g (3½oz) French beans, topped and tailed

2 tbsps of vegetarian oyster sauce

1 tbsp of light soy sauce

Pinch of soft light brown sugar

Pinch of ground white pepper

Dash of toasted sesame oil

1. Heat a wok over a high heat until it starts to smoke and then add the groundnut oil. Add the garlic, ginger, chilli and mushrooms and stir-fry for 1 minute, then add the mock duck and stir-fry for just under a minute. Tip in the broccoli and French beans and stir-fry for a further minute.

2. Season with the remaining ingredients, then remove from the heat and serve immediately with boiled rice.

Specials

In Taiwan, whenever there was a special occasion, my grandmother would spend days in advance preparing the food for it and she would go to town creating a whole range of dishes, whether meat, fish or vegetarian, as well as noodles and desserts – every chapter in this book!

Preparations for the Dragon Boat Festival or *Duan Wu Jie* in Mandarin Chinese – which falls on the fifth day of the fifth month in the lunar calendar and celebrates the life of the legendary poet Chu-Yuan – were a particular labour of love for her. During the festival, *zong-zi* are eaten, a special type of rice dumpling wrapped in bamboo leaves, and my grandmother would make hundreds of these for the family to enjoy.

Just selecting the ingredients for them seemed to take for ever. A week before, my grandfather would be despatched to pick the best dried Chinese mushrooms from the market, along with the freshest shallots and root ginger. Then my grandmother and great-aunts would set to work preparing all the ingredients for the rice parcels. Hours

would be spent soaking the dried mushrooms and you could hear the sound of shallots being endlessly chopped in the days leading up to the festival. Pork belly would be stewed for hours, 'red-cooked' style, with star anise, soy sauce and sugar, until the meat was meltingly tender. Meanwhile, large bamboo steamers full of salted duck-egg yolks would be cooking away on a wooden stove nearby.

All these ingredients would be wok-fried, together with seasoned raw rice, then wrapped in bamboo leaves and steamed for hours until the rice was soft and slightly sticky. When the time finally came, we would devour the dumplings within minutes! I now appreciate all that effort far more than I did as a child.

These days, whenever a family friend gives me some homemade *zong-zi*, I eat them with whole-hearted appreciation because I know just how much labour has gone into making them.

Specials are just that – special. There is nothing more satisfying than seeing your guests enjoy the food you have prepared for them, and nothing more delightful than when someone cooks for you. Happy memories such as these are gold dust: they will touch your heart and stay with you always.

The recipes that follow include some of my favourite special-occasion dishes that I like to serve for family and friends. Some Chinese takeaways serve special dishes, but I notice that most of these are Southeast Asian in origin, such as Thai green chicken curry or Malaysian-style ho fun rice noodles. I would like the specials section to be more varied and offer some Chinese street food as well as 'fu-sian' dishes.

In my fantasy takeaway, I would include dishes such as my Chilli Bean Braised Beef with Coriander and Steamed Mantou, Spiced Lamb Chops with Pickled Onion and Coriander Salad or 'Tiger Bites Pig' with Pickled Cucumber – Chinese-style hamburgers made with Hakka-style Pork Belly (see pages 162, 175 and 171). These dishes are also perfect for entertaining, and don't take too long to prepare. There is a recipe for every occasion here, whether casual or more formal. And they can easily be doubled up for larger gatherings for sharing, along with some simple side dishes.

Chilli bean braised beef with coriander and steamed mantou

Stewed dishes are in my opinion perfect winter food. I love the moreish flavour of slow-cooked beef with soy and chilli bean sauce, so I adapted my Taiwanese-style beef noodles to make a quicker version – a lifesaver for a last-minute dinner party. This dish is served with fluffy mantou, which can be bought from Chinese supermarkets and steamed from frozen. Slightly sweet in taste, these wheat-flour buns are ideal for soaking up the spicy sauce – a perfect balance of flavour and texture.

PREP TIME: 10 minutes • **COOK IN:** 20 minutes • **SERVES:** 2–4 to share

4 frozen mantou buns
1 tbsp of groundnut oil
2 large shallots, chopped
350g (12oz) beef sirloin, cut into 1.5cm (⅝in) cubes
1 tbsp of Shaohsing rice wine or dry sherry
2 spring onions, sliced
1 tbsp of chilli oil (optional)
handful of coriander, roughly chopped

FOR THE SAUCE
100ml (3½fl oz) beef stock
2 tbsps of chilli bean paste
2 tbsps of light soy sauce
1 tsp of dark soy sauce
1 tsp of soft light brown sugar
1 tbsp of runny honey

> **ALSO TRY**
> You could also use stewing beef and slow-cook it. If you can't get hold of mantou, serve with buttered bread rolls instead.

1. Place the mantou in a bamboo steamer lined with greaseproof paper. Set the steamer over a saucepan of boiling water (making sure the bottom of the steamer doesn't touch the water) and steam for 15–20 minutes or until the buns are soft and heated through. Reduce the heat to low and keep the mantou in the steamer until ready to serve.

2. Meanwhile, heat a wok over a high heat until it starts to smoke and add half the groundnut oil. Stir-fry the shallots for 2 minutes or until slightly softened. Scoop the shallots to one side of the wok, add the remaining groundnut oil and tip in the beef.

3. As the beef starts to brown, add the rice wine or dry sherry and stir-fry for 1–2 minutes or until fully browned. Add the spring onions and toss together with the beef, then add all the ingredients for the sauce and cook on a medium heat for 12 minutes or until the beef is tender.

4. Season with the chilli oil (if using), stir in the chopped coriander and serve with the steamed mantou.

Crackling pork shoulder with Chinese spices

This is not your typical takeaway dish, but in China, Hong Kong and Taiwan you have takeaway eateries that sell roast duck and roast pork, as well as various stewed meats, which you can buy and reheat or cook with at home. Most families don't make their own roast meat because they need special ovens and there are rotisseries that do the job just as well. However, I do love roasts, especially on a Sunday (no doubt influenced by my English friends). This one is really easy to cook, making for effortless, fuss-free entertaining. If I had a takeaway, I would install gigantic ovens and roast whole ducks, chickens and joints of pork like this one.

PREP TIME: 10 minutes, plus 15 minutes for resting • **COOK IN:** 40 minutes • **SERVES:** 4

500g (1lb 2oz) boneless pork shoulder

FOR THE SPICE MIX
2 tsps of sea salt
1 tbsp of black peppercorns
1 tbsp of soft light brown sugar
1 tbsp of Chinese five-spice powder
5cm (2in) piece of cassia bark
4 cloves
2 star anise

1. Preheat the oven to 200°C (400°F), gas mark 6.

2. For the spice mix, tip all the ingredients for the spice mix into a mortar and pound with a pestle into a fine powder. Alternatively, grind in a spice grinder, if you have one.

3. Score the surface of the pork fat with a sharp knife (this is to help keep the pork crisp during cooking), then rub the spice mixture over the pork, working it well into the score lines on the fatty side of the meat.

4. Place the pork in a roasting tin and roast in the oven for about 40 minutes or until the juices run clear when the meat is pierced with a knife or skewer. Remove from the oven and allow to rest for 15 minutes before slicing. This tastes delicious with the Sweet Roasted Vegetables (see page 146).

Pork fillet with kimchi and enoki mushrooms

I had a delicious kimchi dish at a Japanese restaurant in Taiwan earlier this year. We had ordered far too much and at the end of the meal my sister-in-law put the leftovers aside to be boxed for takeaway, in the process marrying a stir-fried pork dish with some kimchi (Korean-style fermented vegetables). We had it as a late-night snack when we got back to her house later and ever since then I have been addicted to pork with kimchi. It pays to use a good-quality kimchi – you can buy it from a Chinese supermarket, either in a jar or in a foil pack from the chilled section. And don't forget the enoki mushrooms – they provide a delicious soft, chewy texture and soak up all the juices. If you can't get hold of them, however, just leave them out. This is a fast-wok dish: make sure you work quickly to avoid overcooking the pork fillet.

PREP TIME: 5 minutes • **COOK IN:** 5 minutes • **SERVES:** 2–4 to share

1 tbsp of groundnut oil

2.5cm (1in) piece of root ginger, peeled and sliced into matchsticks

2 pork fillets (300g/11oz in total), cut into 5mm (¼in) slices

1 tbsp of mirin

1 tbsp of light soy sauce

200g (7oz) kimchi

200g (7oz) enoki mushrooms

2 pinches of sea salt

1 tbsp of clear rice vinegar or cider vinegar

2 spring onions, sliced on the diagonal

Drizzle of chilli oil

1. Heat a wok over a high heat until it starts to smoke and then add the groundnut oil. Stir-fry the ginger for a few seconds, then add the pork slices and stir-fry for 2 minutes or until browned at the edges.

2. Add the mirin and soy sauce and cook for 1 minute, then add the kimchi and enoki mushrooms. Season with the salt and vinegar and mix in well. Stir in the spring onions and then drizzle over the chilli oil and serve immediately with jasmine rice.

Chinese sweet pork sausages with garlic

Chinese pork sausages are traditionally made in the month before Chinese New Year when the winter sun dries the meat. My favourite are Taiwanese fresh *xiang chang* sausages, slightly sweet and perfect with boiled rice and stir-fried vegetables. There are several different varieties of sausage: red and white ones are made from pork belly, for instance, while darker ones include liver. You can buy them vacuum-packed from Chinese supermarkets – they keep for weeks in the fridge and can be frozen too. They shouldn't be eaten raw, however, and the best way to prepare them is to steam them.

In this recipe I've steamed the sausages, then pan-fried them and served them with slices of garlic. They could be served as an appetiser or as an accompaniment to a variety of dishes, such as the Fish-fragrant Aubergine with Pork or Yellow Bean Chicken with French Beans and Shiitake Mushrooms (see pages 115 and 78).

PREP TIME: 5 minutes • **COOK IN:** 20 minutes • **SERVES:** 2–4 to share

2 dried Chinese pork sausages

1 tbsp of groundnut oil

2 cloves of garlic, very thinly sliced

3 sprigs of coriander, to garnish

1. Place the sausages on a heatproof plate in a bamboo steamer, cover with the lid and set over a saucepan or wok of boiling water. Steam for 15 minutes (making sure the bottom of the steamer doesn't touch the water), then remove from the heat and rest for 2 minutes in the basket. Take the sausages out of the steamer and cut on the diagonal into 5mm (¼in) slices.

2. Heat a wok over a high heat until it starts to smoke and then add the groundnut oil. Tip in the slices of sausage and stir-fry for 2 minutes, then transfer to a serving plate, alternating the slices of sausage with the garlic. Serve immediately, garnished with the sprigs of coriander.

> **ALSO TRY**
> You could try serving the sausage as they do in China, with the garlic on the side. The idea is to eat a slice of sausage with a slice of raw garlic.

Hakka-style pork belly

In traditional Hakka cuisine, this dish is known as *mei cai ko rou*. The meat is steamed with some fermented dried cabbage in a soy-flavoured cooking liquid, which gives the dish a salty as well as sweet, earthy flavour. I like to serve the pork belly Western-style, with stir-fried savoy cabbage and mashed potato. Or you could always use it for making my Chinese-style 'hamburger' on page 171.

PREP TIME: 10 minutes • **COOK IN:** 1¾ hours • **SERVES:** 4

3 pieces of pork belly
  (650g/1lb 7oz in total),
  skin on

2 tbsps of groundnut oil

1 tbsp of dark soy sauce

2.5cm (1in) piece of root
  ginger, peeled and sliced
  into matchsticks

1 tbsp of Sichuan peppercorns

1 tsp of cornflour mixed with
  1 tbsp of water

FOR THE SAUCE

2 star anise

100ml (3½fl oz) vegetable
  stock

4 tbsps of light soy sauce

1 tbsp of Shaohsing rice wine
  or dry sherry

2 tsps of soft light brown
  sugar

> **ALSO TRY**
> If you're watching your waistline and prefer a leaner cut of pork, use pork loins instead of belly.

1. Bring a large saucepan of water to the boil and add the pork pieces. Bring back up to the boil, then reduce the heat and simmer for 30 minutes. Drain the pork and dry on kitchen paper.

2. Meanwhile, add all the ingredients for the sauce to a jug or bowl and stir together.

3. Heat a wok over a high heat until it starts to smoke and then add half the groundnut oil. Add the pork pieces and season with the soy sauce, then fry the meat for 1 minute on each side or until browned. Remove the pork and transfer to a heatproof dish that will fit inside a large bamboo steamer.

4. Place the wok back over a high heat and add the remaining groundnut oil. Add the ginger and Sichuan peppercorns and stir-fry for a few seconds and then add the sauce, bringing it the boil. Remove from the heat and pour over the pork in the steamer.

5. Place the steamer over a pan of boiling water (making sure that the bottom of the steamer doesn't touch the water) and steam the pork in the sauce on a medium heat for 1 hour.

6. Remove the meat from the steamer and pour the juices into a small wok or saucepan, bring to the boil and then add the cornflour paste to thicken the sauce. Cut the pork into 5cm (2in) slices, pour over the sauce and serve immediately.

'Tiger bites pig' (Chinese hamburgers) with pickled cucumber

Known as *gua bao* ('pork belly buns') in Taiwan, this dish also goes by the name of 'Tiger Bites Pig' because the sliced bun looks like a tiger's mouth with a 'pig' (or piece of pork belly) in it! *Gua bao* typically consists of Hakka-style Pork Belly (see page 168) sandwiched in a steamed wheat-flour bun, sprinkled with ground peanuts and sugar and served with salted fermented cabbage. For this version of the dish, I've simply substituted the fermented cabbage with pickled cucumbers and the *gua bao* buns with mantou.

Deliciously fluffy and sweet, mantou are usually eaten for breakfast but go really well in this recipe. You can buy them from the frozen section of a Chinese supermarket, although some specialist outlets sell the actual *gua bao* buns, ready sliced, if you'd like to try those instead.

PREP TIME: 10 minutes, plus 20 minutes for marinating • **COOK IN:** 15–20 minutes • **SERVES:** 4

5 tbsps of roasted peanuts

2 tbsps of granulated sugar

4 frozen mantou buns

4 slices of warm freshly cooked Hakka-style Pork Belly (see page 168)

Small handful of chopped coriander, to garnish

FOR THE PICKLED CUCUMBER

½ cucumber (unpeeled), halved lengthways and finely sliced

1 tbsp of clear rice vinegar or cider vinegar

1 tbsp of mirin

Pinch of salt

Pinch of soft brown sugar

1. Place all the ingredients for the pickled cucumber in a bowl, stir together, cover and leave to marinate for 20 minutes. Put the peanuts in a mortar and crush with a pestle to a fine powder, or use a spice grinder, then mix with the sugar.

2. While the pickled cucumber is marinating, place the mantou in a bamboo steamer lined with greaseproof paper. Set the steamer over a saucepan of boiling water (making sure the bottom of the steamer doesn't touch the water) and steam for 15–20 minutes or until the buns are soft and heated through.

3. Slice each bun in half, place a piece of pork belly inside and drizzle over some of the cooking juices. Add some of the pickled cucumber, sprinkle over a little of the peanut and sugar mixture and garnish with some chopped coriander.

Roast pork brioche buns with caramelised red onions

These are ideal for children's parties and make a change from boring sandwiches. They would also be great for a summer barbecue. The pork can be marinated in advance and then quickly cooked and sandwiched in the brioche buns just before serving.

PREP TIME: 10 minutes, plus 20 minutes for marinating • **COOK IN:** 10 minutes • **SERVES:** 4

500g (1lb 2oz) pork fillet
1 tbsp of groundnut oil
1 tbsp of runny honey
4 small brioche buns
4 Red Gem lettuce leaves

FOR THE MARINADE
1 clove of garlic, crushed and finely chopped
2 tbsps of yellow bean sauce
1 tbsp of Shaohsing rice wine or dry sherry
1 tbsp of light soy sauce
1 tbsp of groundnut oil

FOR THE CARAMELISED RED ONIONS
1 tbsp of groundnut oil
1 red onion, finely sliced
1 tbsp of soft light brown sugar

1. Put all the ingredients for the marinade into a large bowl and stir together. Add the pork fillet and turn in the mixture to coat, then cover and place in the fridge to marinate for at least 20 minutes.

2. Remove the pork from the marinade (retaining this) and cut into 5mm (¼in) slices. Heat a wok over a high heat until it starts to smoke and then add the groundnut oil. Add the pork slices and stir-fry for 2 minutes.

3. Stir the honey into the marinade, then add to the pork and cook for another 2 minutes or until the meat has acquired a slightly sticky glaze. Transfer to a plate and leave to rest.

4. Meanwhile, make the caramelised red onions. Heat a small wok over a medium-high heat until it starts to smoke and then add the groundnut oil. Add the onion slices and cook for 3 minutes or until softened, then sprinkle over the sugar and cook for a further 1–2 minutes or until sticky and caramelised.

5. Slice each bun in half, add a lettuce leaf, some fried pork slices and a spoonful of caramelised onions and serve immediately.

Spiced lamb chops with pickled onion and coriander salad

This dish takes its inspiration from the spices used by the Muslim Chinese in their cuisine. Their ancestors would have travelled to China along the Silk Road, bringing their own customs and cooking styles, including spicy lamb kebabs, which can now be purchased from food stalls and takeaways across the country. I've taken my cue from them for this dish, in which the lamb is first marinated in a spice paste and then cooked in a wok. It's fast, simple, delicious and healthy, as well as perfect for entertaining.

PREP TIME: 10 minutes, plus 20 minutes for marinating • **COOK IN:** 5 minutes • **SERVES:** 2

4 lamb chops
1 tbsp of groundnut oil
Salt and ground white pepper

FOR THE SPICE PASTE
1 tbsp of groundnut oil
2 green chillies, sliced
1 tsp of dried chilli flakes
1 tsp of medium curry powder
1 tsp of turmeric
1 tsp of ground cumin
1 tbsp of Shaohsing rice wine
   or dry sherry

FOR THE SALAD
1 white onion, sliced into rings
Juice of ½ lemon
4 tbsps of clear rice vinegar or
   cider vinegar
1 tbsp of mirin
¼ tsp of salt
¼ tsp of caster sugar
Small handful of coriander,
   finely chopped

1. Place the onion rings for the salad in a bowl with the lemon juice and 400ml (14fl oz) of water and leave to marinate for 10 minutes.

2. Meanwhile, put all the ingredients for the spice paste in another bowl and mix together well. Add the lamb chops and turn in the paste to coat, then cover with cling film and leave to marinate for 20 minutes.

3. Drain the onions rings well, then place in a clean bowl with all the remaining ingredients for the salad except the coriander, stir together to combine and set aside to marinate for 10–15 minutes. Sprinkle over the coriander just before serving.

4. Heat a wok over a high heat until it starts to smoke and then add the groundnut oil. Add the marinated lamb chops and fry for 2 minutes on each side. (Fry for another 1–2 minutes if you prefer them well done.)

5. Season further, to taste, with salt and ground white pepper and serve with the pickled onion and coriander salad.

Cantonese-style steamed lobster with ginger soy sauce

This recipe is inspired by the Cantonese way of serving steamed fish – lightly dressed in a hot ginger soy oil that allows the fresh sweet flavour of the fish to come through. I decided to try it with lobster and it works really well – perfect for a romantic dinner for two. Try serving it with stir-fried vegetables and some Egg and Asparagus Fried Rice (see page 186).

PREP TIME: 10 minutes, plus 30 minutes for chilling • **COOK IN:** 12 minutes • **SERVES:** 2

1 live lobster

2 spring onions, sliced lengthways

Handful of coriander sprigs

FOR THE GINGER SOY SAUCE

2 tbsps of groundnut oil

1 tbsp of peeled and grated root ginger

4 tbsps of light soy sauce

1 tbsp of toasted sesame oil

1. First place the lobster in the freezer for 30 minutes. Remove from the freezer and quickly slice through the head with a sharp knife, then slice the lobster in half lengthways, retaining the head.

2. Lay the lobster halves shell side down on a heatproof plate and place inside a large bamboo steamer. Cover the steamer with the lid and set over a wok or saucepan filled with boiling water, making sure the bottom of the steamer does not touch the water.

3. Steam over a high heat for 10 minutes, then take off the heat. Remove the lid and drape the spring onions and coriander sprigs over the top of the lobster, then replace the lid to allow the herbs to wilt and soften in the steam. Keep the lobster in the steamer until ready to serve.

4. Next make the ginger soy sauce. Heat a small wok over a high heat until it starts to smoke and then add the groundnut oil. Add the ginger and stir-fry quickly for a few seconds, then add the soy sauce and toasted sesame oil and bring to the boil. Remove the wok from the heat.

5. Remove the lid from the steamer, pour the hot sauce over the lobster and serve immediately in the bamboo steamer basket.

Clams and Chinese sausage with bean sprouts and spring onions

I love clams and Chinese sausages, so I decided to pair the two and the result is a fragrant, sweet and savoury dish. The bean sprouts add texture and soak up the flavour of the gingery, winey sauce. Very Chinese in taste, it is good served with some plain boiled rice.

PREP TIME: 15 minutes • **COOK IN:** 7 minutes • **SERVES:** 2–4 to share

300g (11oz) clams

1 tbsp of groundnut oil

2.5cm (1in) piece of root ginger, peeled and sliced into matchsticks

100g (3½oz) cooked Chinese sausage (see page 167), cut into 5mm (¼in) slices

1 tbsp of Shaohsing rice wine or dry sherry

100ml (3½fl oz) vegetable stock

1 tbsp of light soy sauce

1 tbsp of cornflour mixed with 1 tbsp of water

Large handful of bean sprouts

1 spring onion, cut on the diagonal into 1cm (½in) slices

Sprig of coriander, to garnish (optional)

1. First scrub the clams, removing any bits of debris from the shells and discarding any that remain open when tapped against a hard surface.

2. Heat a wok over a high heat until it starts to smoke and then add the groundnut oil. Add the ginger and stir-fry for a few seconds, then add the pieces of cooked Chinese sausage and stir-fry for a few seconds more. Add the clams and cook for 1 minute.

3. As the shells start to open, add the rice wine or dry sherry, then pour in the vegetable stock. Bring to the boil, then reduce the heat and cook for 3–4 minutes or until all the shells have opened. Discard any that remain closed.

4. Season with the soy sauce, then add the cornflour paste, stir in the bean sprouts and spring onion and cook for 1 minute to allow the sauce to thicken. Transfer to a serving dish, garnish with a sprig of coriander, if you like, and serve immediately.

Rice

Rice is the most important staple food for a huge proportion of the world's population. It is eaten all over the world and is cultivated in the continents of Asia, Australia, America and Africa. In China, we have a greeting, '*Ni chi fan le mei you?*' ('Have you eaten?' in Mandarin Chinese), in which the word '*fan*' means both 'cooked rice' and 'food'. Not only is 'rice' synonymous with 'food', but as food and eating are at the forefront of people's minds, the word has evolved into part of a common everyday greeting!

In ancient China, wild rice first grew along the valleys of the fertile Yangtze River. It soon became domesticated and has been cultivated for thousands of years, with over 40,000 different varieties being grown. The most common form of rice is long grain, but there are also short-grain varieties, such as glutinous or 'sticky' rice.

Many people ask me what is the best type of rice for Chinese cooking and I say just choose the one you like best. Long-grain rice like basmati is delicious, but for frying I prefer shorter-grained varieties that contain a bit more amylopectin, a type of starch that makes the rice stickier. My favourite is jasmine rice from Thailand, with its nutty-coconut aroma. I like to serve highly flavoured dishes with jasmine rice. In my view, it makes the perfect accompaniment to many Chinese dishes. I mostly boil or steam it. I would only fry it to use up any leftover rice, and on the odd occasions when I have a craving for fried rice, I deliberately make more rice the night before to ensure I have plenty left over to cook with the next day. This is a technique I learned from my grandmother and mother – two kitchen gurus that could turn any leftovers, including rice, into the most amazing dishes.

I love the way freshly cooked rice grains, fluffy but still a bit al dente, absorb the flavours of dishes so well. As a child, I used to stain my rice with the sauces of my grandmother's dishes, whether it was a dressing made with oil, ginger, spring onion and chilli or the dark-reddish sauce of red-cooked pig's trotters or Pork Rib, Turnip and Carrot Broth with Coriander (see page 134), a recipe handed down from my great-grandfather. (He had no teeth and would need to moisten the rice to make it into a watery congee so that it was easier for him to eat.)

The smell of jasmine rice cooking always reminds me of my grandmother's kitchen. I would know when it was time to eat when I could smell that delicate sweet fragrance in the air and hear the click of our Tatung rice cooker (my grandmother's favourite modern tool) switch from 'cook' to 'warm'. My grandmother would then tell one of my great-aunts to fluff up the rice with an old bamboo spatula to 'air' the grains before we formed a queue to spoon it into our bowls.

I have a huge extended family, and even though my grandparents lived on farmland, they were considered quite wealthy. (My grandfather always boasted that we were one of the first families in the village to own a fridge, rice cooker and TV.) My grandfather is one of 11 siblings and together they own a bamboo farm, orangery and a number of sweet potato patches. Since they all lived together, my great-aunts and great-uncles would eat together. Every mealtime was a banquet, with my grandmother at the helm as head chef with rotating sous chefs, usually my second great-aunt, as she lived next door and was always on hand. Sometimes leftover rice from the dinner the evening before would be turned into congee for breakfast the next morning. My grandmother would heat up some water in her large wok on her wood-fired stove. Once the water 'opened' (i.e. boiled), she would pour the rice in and stir, breaking it up in the hot water. She would boil the congee for a while until the starch from the rice broke down, creating a thick white porridge. Meanwhile, to accompany the congee, she would lay out small plates of mini pickled cucumbers, 'stinky' fermented bean curd (*dofu ru* or *dao-ru* in Taiwanese) in soy sauce, pickled young tender bamboo shoots in chilli oil, dried pork floss, salted fried red peanuts and sheets of dried seaweed. She would also put out either boiled salted duck eggs or make fried eggs seasoned with soy sauce (see page 18 for my version of this dish!). Even now, in my Western kitchen, the smell of rice cooking transports me back to Taiwan and to memories of Pai He.

Rice, however it's cooked, is a magical ingredient and to me much more than just an accompaniment. Cooked rice is also perhaps the most popular side dish on the takeaway menu, especially in its fried form. With saltier or spicier dishes, I would usually recommend plain boiled rice or a light egg-fried rice like my Egg and Asparagus Fried Rice (see page 186). For lighter main dishes, you could serve a meatier fried rice, such as my version of Yangzhou Fried Rice (see page 188), which also makes a great brunch dish served on its own. However you like to serve rice, I hope there are a few dishes here to inspire you to try your own variations at home.

Boiled jasmine rice

In China and Taiwan, much of the rice that is cultivated is not exported. The variety used in Britain that is most similar to Chinese rice is jasmine rice, originally from Thailand. It is also a favourite of mine, with its fragrant, delicious aroma, and one of my staple store-cupboard ingredients.

PREP TIME: 2 minutes • **COOK IN:** 15–20 minutes • **SERVES:** 4 to share

350g (12oz) jasmine rice, rinsed until the water runs clear

1. Place the rice in a large heavy-based saucepan and add 600ml (1 pint) of water. Bring to the boil, then cover with a tight-fitting lid, turn the heat down to low and cook for 15–20 minutes or until all the water has been absorbed. Uncover the pan and remove from the heat. Fluff up the grains with a fork and serve immediately.

Fragrant star anise rice

When I was young, my grandmother often made 'oiled' rice, a sticky rice moistened with soy pork drippings from pork cooked in star anise and soy sauce. When I am in search of those flavours, I cook the rice with some chicken or vegetable stock, in addition to the soy sauce and star anise, for a version that is lighter and healthier but still full of flavour and aroma.

(if using vegetable stock) **PREP TIME:** 5 minutes • **COOK IN:** 15–20 minutes • **SERVES:** 4 to share

350g (12oz) jasmine rice, rinsed until the water runs clear
300ml (½ pint) vegetable or chicken stock
1 star anise
1 tbsp of light soy sauce

1. Place the rice in a large heavy-based saucepan and add the stock and 300ml (½ pint) of water. Bring to the boil, add the star anise and soy sauce, then cover with a tight-fitting lid, turn the heat down to low and cook for 15–20 minutes or until all the liquid has been absorbed. Uncover the pan and remove from the heat. Fluff up the grains with a fork and serve immediately.

Egg and asparagus fried rice

The first time I tried to make egg-fried rice, I made the mistake of frying rice that was freshly cooked and really moist. The result was a thick congealed porridge of egg and spring onions – disaster! I was only 11 and so my father ate it anyway. To master fried rice, check that the wok is hot enough and use leftover cooked rice if possible. If using freshly cooked rice, make sure it's al dente rather than too soft. Make sure there is enough oil in the wok too, and try not to stab at the rice but toss it in the wok as it fries. This is my classic egg-fried rice recipe, to which I like to add blanched sliced baby asparagus when in season, although frozen peas would work just as well.

PREP TIME: 5 minutes • **COOK IN:** 8 minutes • **SERVES:** 4 to share

100g (3½oz) baby asparagus spears, woody ends snapped off

Salt and ground white pepper

1 tbsp of groundnut oil

2 eggs, lightly beaten

350g (12oz) cold leftover cooked jasmine rice or freshly cooked long-grain rice (see the tips below)

2 tbsps of light soy sauce

1 tbsp of toasted sesame oil

1 large spring onion, finely sliced

1. Blanch the asparagus spears in a saucepan of boiling salted water for 3 minutes, then drain and refresh in cold water. Slice the cooked asparagus crossways into 5mm (¼in) pieces and set aside.

2. Heat a wok over a high heat until it starts to smoke and then add the groundnut oil. Add the eggs and stir for 2 minutes to scramble, then tip in the rice and stir well in the wok to break it up. Add the blanched asparagus pieces and toss together well.

3. Season with the soy sauce, toasted sesame oil and salt and pepper to taste. Add the spring onion and mix well, then remove from the heat and serve immediately.

CHING'S TIPS

If cooking rice to use later, make sure the cooked rice is cooled for no longer than 30 minutes at room temperature, then transfer to a bowl or plastic box, cover and keep refrigerated until ready to use. Only reheat/cook rice once after it has been cooked already.

If using freshly cooked rice for a fried dish, try a long-grain variety such as basmati. For this dish, use 175g (6oz) of uncooked long-grain rice (well rinsed) and boil in 350ml (12fl oz) of water until all the water is absorbed. This will increase the cooking time by 20 minutes.

Ching's Yangzhou fried rice

This recipe from eastern China traditionally includes pieces of smoked Chinese ham, as well as egg, shiitake mushrooms, prawns and crabmeat. The result is a rich and elegant dish that has evolved into a Chinese takeaway classic all over the world. When making it at home, I like the combination of Cantonese pork with baby prawns and mixed vegetables, although you can vary this dish endlessly, using whatever vegetables you have to hand or just a handful of peas.

PREP TIME: 10 minutes • **COOK IN:** 5 minutes • **SERVES:** 2–4 to share

2 tbsps of groundnut oil

3 eggs, beaten

50g (2oz) cooked shelled baby prawns

50g (2oz) mixed vegetables (peas, mini broccoli florets, sweetcorn kernels and grated carrot)

50g (2oz) roast pork, diced

50g (2oz) cooked chicken, shredded (optional)

400g (14oz) cold leftover cooked jasmine rice (see the first tip on page 186) or freshly cooked long-grain rice (see the tip below)

2 tbsps of light soy sauce

2 tbsps of toasted sesame oil

Pinch of salt

2 pinches of ground white pepper

Sprigs of coriander, to garnish (optional)

1. Heat a wok over a high heat until it starts to smoke and then add half the groundnut oil. Pour in the beaten eggs and leave to settle for 1–2 minutes, then swirl around the wok and, using a wooden spoon, stir the eggs to lightly scramble them. Transfer to a plate and set aside.

2. Reheat the wok and add the remaining groundnut oil. Tip in the prawns and mixed vegetables and stir-fry for less than 1 minute. Add the roast pork and cooked chicken (if using) and stir-fry for just under a minute. Add the cooked rice and mix well to break it down in the wok.

3. Return the scrambled eggs to the wok and season with the soy sauce, toasted sesame oil, salt and pepper, then remove from the heat and serve immediately, garnished with coriander sprigs, if you like.

CHING'S TIP
If using freshly cooked rice, take 200g (7oz) of uncooked long-grain rice, such as basmati, rinse it well and then boil in 400ml (14fl oz) of water, cooking it until all the water has been absorbed. This will increase the cooking time by 20 minutes.

ALSO TRY
You could include other types of cooked meat in this dish, such as chunks of honey-roast ham instead of the chicken.

Chinese fruity roast duck and wild rice salad

When I was running my kitchen, I had to develop recipes all the time. There was one particular dish that was packed so full of flavour and was so popular with my customers that I have shared it here with you. It is my version of Chinese-style roast duck salad, to which I've added many twists, including the nutty soy dressing.

PREP TIME: 10 minutes, plus 40 minutes for cooling/chilling
COOK IN: 20–25 minutes • **SERVES:** 2–4 to share

200g (7oz) brown basmati rice

100g (3½oz) wild black rice

300g (11oz) roast duck (see page 70), shredded

1 cucumber (unpeeled), deseeded and diced

1 red pepper, deseeded and diced

Small handful each of pomegranate seeds, crushed walnuts, chopped dried apricots and chopped dried cranberries

Small handful each of finely chopped coriander leaves and finely shredded mint

2 spring onions, finely sliced

Handful of watercress and baby spinach leaves, to serve

FOR THE DRESSING

3 tbsps of extra-virgin olive oil

1 tsp of peeled and grated root ginger

2 tbsps of light soy sauce

1 tbsp of toasted sesame oil

1 tbsp of clear rice vinegar or cider vinegar

Pinch of salt and black pepper

1. Place both types of rice in a large heavy-based saucepan and add 600ml (1 pint) of water. Bring to the boil, then cover with a tight-fitting lid, turn the heat down to low and cook for 20–25 minutes or until the rice is al dente and all the water has been absorbed.

2. Uncover the pan and remove from the heat, then fluff up the grains with a fork and tip into a bowl. Let the rice stand for 20 minutes to cool down, and then cover and refrigerate for at least 20 minutes, or preferably a few hours, until well chilled.

3. Shortly before serving, toss together all the remaining ingredients for the salad with the chilled rice in a large bowl. Place the dressing ingredients in a jug or bowl, stir well and then add to the salad, tossing the salad ingredients together so that they are well coated. Serve on a bed of the watercress and baby spinach leaves.

Classic plain congee

Although in my family congee or rice porridge (*zhou* in Mandarin Chinese) is eaten mainly for breakfast or lunch, it can also be served for dinner. It doesn't usually feature on takeaway menus in the West, but eateries in China regularly serve it for breakfast. If I had a takeaway restaurant, I would serve congee in soup cartons as a restorative – it makes a great cure for hangovers and other ailments. Whenever I had an upset stomach, my grandmother would give me a steaming bowl of salted congee and I would feel I could live to see another day!

Congee traditionally consists of two types of short-grain rice, including some glutinous rice for a stickier thicker consistency. If you have some glutinous rice in your cupboard, then by all means include it as a fifth of the total quantity stated below. Otherwise using just jasmine rice will be fine.

PREP TIME: 5 minutes • **COOK IN:** 65 minutes • **SERVES:** 4–6 to share

250g (9oz) jasmine rice or 200g (7oz) jasmine rice mixed with 50g (2oz) glutinous rice, rinsed until the water runs clear

250ml (9fl oz) vegetable stock

1. Pour the rice into a large heavy-based saucepan, add the stock and 700ml (1¼ pints) of water and bring to the boil. Once boiled, reduce the heat to medium-low, place a tight-fitting lid on the pan and cook for just over an hour, stirring occasionally to make sure the rice does not stick to the sides and the bottom of the pan, until the rice breaks down into a thick porridge.

2. Remove the pan from the heat and serve the congee plain as an accompaniment, or seasoned with a little salt if you have stomach ache!

CHING'S TIP
If you prefer a thinner, more watery porridge, simply add extra hot, boiled water as the rice cooks.

ALSO TRY
You can add all sorts of different ingredients to the congee once it's cooked, such as cooked green or split yellow mung beans or different types of meat and shellfish (see page 25 for a few ideas).

Noodles

I have always loved noodles. Dried noodles are one of my favourite store-cupboard ingredients to reach for when hunger pangs strike and I need a quick fix. And I love noodles in whatever shape or form, whether made with rice or with wheat.

Noodles were always eaten in my family on birthdays. A birthday meal would consist of *misua*, very fine wheat-flour noodles (a bit like vermicelli) tossed in toasted sesame oil, garlic and a little salt. When cooked, these noodles bundle up and stick together, and never break up unless you do the breaking; they are extremely fine and delicate, yet full of 'spring' or 'al-dente-ness'.

In China, these uncut noodles symbolise longevity and that is why we eat them on festive occasions. It is my father's favourite dish, and whenever he has an upset stomach he asks for *misua*. The funny thing is that, having lived in England for all these years, my family would now buy a large cream cake to celebrate a birthday, but it would be reserved for dessert; we'd still have *misua* for the first course. A union of opposites, you might say: a simple savoury dish followed by an extravagant pudding – so East and West.

If I had to choose between rice and noodles, it would have to be noodles. I am obsessed with them, even more so after running my own food business. In fact, it was my love of noodles that inspired me to set up Fuge. It was passing a sandwich chain serving bland wheat-flour noodles at £3.50 a box that showed me where my destiny lay. Life for me was not in a box of chocolates (to adapt a line from *Forrest Gump*) but a carton of *liang mein* ('cool noodles').

At the time, sushi had just taken off in Britain and I thought noodles might go down well too. I have always had a passion for *liang mein*, having bought it many times from snack stalls on the streets of Taipei: slippery chilled egg noodles served with grated carrots and cucumber in a spicy garlic and sesame dressing – that was my usual.

It was April 1999, my final year at university. While everyone else was applying for internships at large banks and accountancy firms, I picked up the phone and dialled all the supermarket chains I could, to try to book appointments with their buyers. I was desperate. After years of surviving by the skin of my teeth, I needed to turn my life around.

I tried making appointments with several supermarkets, including the one whose noodles I thought were awful, and they all turned me down except one – a small independent chain. I persuaded the buyer to book a meeting and showed up with a container of my homemade noodle salad, a few drawings and an empty salad box. He asked me whether I had a kitchen, a health and hygiene certificate, distribution,

product, pricing, marketing … To all these questions I said no. I could tell by the look on his face that he was not impressed.

But he took pity on me too, giving me a great long list of things I would need to set up in business. I wrote everything down and over the next few months, in the midst of revising for my finals, I gathered together all I would need and went back to him, having found a kitchen, three months' free rent and a distributor just around the corner and with my first HACCP (Hazard Analysis and Critical Control Points) report. I could tell he wasn't expecting to see me, but he loved my 'cool noodle' recipe and decided to give me a break.

At the beginning sales were poor – nobody wanted to eat noodles cold; people thought they should be heated. It was a hard time convincing customers, but I explained that if you eat pasta cold, in salads, the same principle can be applied to noodles.

I started experimenting with different types of noodle – udon, mung bean, buckwheat and rice – and found suppliers who would provide them, and when orders went up I started importing my own range from Taiwan.

The business survived for nearly nine years thanks to the help and support of family, friends and most of all my customers, who had a passion for good-quality noodles. I even ended up supplying the very people who first rejected my phone calls.

Those were very stressful times and for nearly ten years that was my life. I worked 12-hour days for six days a week; I would see buyers in the morning, then cook the products myself, boxing each dish individually with the help of a few staff. I worked like this for three years while building the business. Sometimes I look back and wonder how on earth I ever did it.

But treading that road has led me to where I am now. To think it all started with a box of takeaway noodles …

Ching's life-changing Taiwanese liang mein

This is one of my favourite snacks. It should be garlicky, spicy, salty and slightly vinegary – very refreshing when served cold on a hot summer's day.

PREP TIME: 10 minutes, plus 20 minutes for chilling • **COOK IN:** 4 minutes • **SERVES:** 2

150g (5oz) dried white shi wheat-flour noodles or medium egg noodles
1 tbsp of toasted sesame oil
Large handful of bean sprouts (optional)
½ cucumber (unpeeled), deseeded and grated
1 carrot, grated
Pinch of hot chilli powder

FOR THE DRESSING
2 cloves of garlic, minced
2 tbsps of sesame paste or tahini
2 tbsps of light soy sauce
2 tbsps of clear rice vinegar or cider vinegar
1 tsp of chilli sauce (optional)

1. Cook the noodles in a saucepan of boiling water for 2–3 minutes until al dente, or according to the instructions on the packet. Drain, then rinse under cold running water and drain again. Drizzle with the toasted sesame oil and toss together to prevent the noodles from sticking to each other. Set aside to allow to cool.

2. Meanwhile, add the bean sprouts (if using) to another saucepan of boiling water and blanch for 30 seconds. Drain and refresh under cold running water, then set aside.

3. On two plates, arrange the salad ingredients in layers – noodles, grated cucumber, grated carrot and bean sprouts (if using) – then cover in cling film and place in the fridge to chill for 20 minutes.

4. Just before serving, mix all the dressing ingredients together in a jug or bowl, then drizzle over the noodle salad and mix together well. Sprinkle with the chilli powder and serve immediately.

Chicken chow mein

Chow mein – which means 'stir-fried noodles' – is one of a large number of noodle dishes. Less familiar dishes might include *e-mein*, Cantonese-style noodles, served with a sauce, and *lo-mein*, containing vegetables and meat or seafood and also served with a sauce.

Chicken chow mein is a takeaway classic. It's also my favourite chow mein dish. This is my version of it, one that I find myself making again and again; it's so good, in fact, that I had to include it.

PREP TIME: 10 minutes • **COOK IN:** 10 minutes • **SERVES:** 2

150g (5oz) dried yellow shi wheat-flour noodles or medium egg noodles

2 dashes of toasted sesame oil

300g (11oz) skinless chicken breasts, sliced into strips

Dash of dark soy sauce

1 tsp of Chinese five-spice powder

1 tsp of chilli sauce (optional)

1 tbsp of cornflour

1–2 tbsps of groundnut oil

1 red pepper, deseeded and finely sliced

150g (5oz) bean sprouts

1 large spring onion, sliced lengthways

2 tbsps of light soy sauce

Ground black pepper

1. Cook the noodles in a saucepan of boiling water for 2–3 minutes until al dente, or according to the instructions on the packet. Drain, then rinse under cold running water and drain again. Drizzle with a dash of sesame oil and toss together to prevent the noodles from sticking to each other.

2. Place the chicken strips in a bowl and season with the dark soy sauce, five-spice powder and chilli sauce (if using). Mix well, then lightly dust the chicken strips with the cornflour.

3. Heat a wok over a high heat until it starts to smoke and add the groundnut oil, then add the chicken pieces and stir-fry for 3–4 minutes or until the chicken is cooked through and golden.

4. Tip in the red pepper and stir-fry for 1 minute, then add the bean sprouts and spring onion and stir-fry for 30 seconds. Stir in the cooked noodles and season with the light soy sauce, the remaining dash of toasted sesame oil and some freshly ground black pepper. Divide the noodles between plates and serve immediately.

Char siu roast pork noodle soup

Cantonese-style roast pork, or *char siu* – literally 'fork roast', from the traditional method of cooking strips of pork on long forks over an open fire – is just the best ingredient to have in the kitchen. If you have enough time at the weekend, it pays to roast pork in this way. You can then use it over the next few days for sandwiches or noodle soups such as this one.

PREP TIME: 10 minutes, plus 20 minutes for marinating • **COOK IN:** 20 minutes • **SERVES:** 2

2 pork fillets
200g (7oz) dried udon (flat wheat-flour) noodles
1 tbsp of toasted sesame oil
600ml (1 pint) vegetable stock
2 small pak choy, leaves separated
1 spring onion, finely sliced
2 small handfuls of bean sprouts

FOR THE MARINADE
2 cloves of garlic, finely chopped
1 tbsp of peeled and grated root ginger
2 tbsps of yellow bean sauce
2 tbsps of runny honey
2 tbsps of light soy sauce
2 tbsps of Shaohsing rice wine or dry sherry
½ tsp of dark soy sauce
2 tbsps of groundnut oil

1. Put all the ingredients for the marinade into a bowl and stir to combine. Add the pork and turn to coat, then cover the bowl and leave to marinate for 20 minutes.

2. In the meantime, preheat the oven to 200°C (400°F), gas mark 6.

3. Heat a griddle pan or frying pan on a high heat, and when it begins to smoke, cook the pork for 2 minutes on each side or until the outside edges are glazed and sticky. Transfer the pork to a roasting tin and roast in the oven for 12 minutes. Leave to rest for 5 minutes and then slice.

4. Meanwhile, cook the noodles in a saucepan of boiling water for 2–3 minutes until al dente, or according to the instructions on the packet. Drain, then rinse under cold running water and drain again. Drizzle with the toasted sesame oil and toss together to prevent the noodles from sticking to each other.

5. Pour the vegetable stock into a separate saucepan and bring to the boil. Add the pak choy leaves and sliced spring onion and remove from the heat.

6. Divide the cooked noodles between two bowls, add a handful of bean sprouts to each bowl and ladle over the soup stock with the pak choy leaves and spring onion. Top with the sliced roast pork and serve immediately.

Singapore noodles

I used to think this was a lengthy recipe, but these days supermarkets have all the ingredients ready-prepared – from cooked chicken breast, shelled tiger prawns to diced bacon, mixed shredded stir-fry vegetables and even cooked vermicelli rice noodles. All you have to do is heat the wok, add the ingredients and season them – it takes no time at all!

PREP TIME: 15 minutes • **COOK IN:** 7 minutes • **SERVES:** 2

2 tbsps of groundnut oil

1 tbsp of peeled and grated root ginger

1 red chilli, deseeded and finely chopped

5 shiitake mushrooms, sliced

1–2 tbsps of turmeric

175g (6oz) raw shelled and deveined tiger prawns

100g (3½oz) smoked bacon, cut into lardons

1 red pepper, deseeded and sliced

1 carrot, cut into matchsticks

Handful of bean sprouts

100g (3½oz) cooked chicken breast, shredded

250g (9oz) dried vermicelli rice noodles, soaked in hot water for 10 minutes and drained

1 tsp of dried chilli flakes

2 tbsps of light soy sauce

2 tbsps of oyster sauce

1 tbsp of clear rice vinegar or cider vinegar

1 egg, beaten

Dash of toasted sesame oil

2 spring onions, sliced lengthways

1. Heat a wok over a high heat until it starts to smoke. Add the groundnut oil and stir-fry the ginger, chilli, mushrooms and turmeric for a few seconds.

2. Add the prawns and stir-fry for 1 minute or until they start to turn pink, then add the bacon and cook for less than 1 minute. Tip in the rest of the vegetables and cook for a further minute, then add the cooked chicken and stir well to combine.

3. Add the noodles and stir-fry for 2 minutes, then season with the chilli flakes, soy sauce, oyster sauce and vinegar, and stir to combine.

4. Add the beaten egg, stirring gently until the egg is cooked through (just under a minute), and then season with the toasted sesame oil. Sprinkle with the spring onions and serve immediately.

ALSO TRY
Instead of the bacon lardons, you could use diced char siu roast pork (see page 198), adding it with the shredded cooked chicken.

Ching's zha jiang noodles

Zha jiang ('fried sauce') noodles are a street-hawker snack, consisting of wheat-flour noodles mixed in a meat sauce. There are many different regional variations, however. In Sichuan, for example, they spice up the dish with Sichuan peppercorns or dried chillies. In Taiwan, they serve the noodles in a little broth with baby leeks or spring onions. My mother likes to add pork and bamboo shoots.

I came to make my own version, using leftovers I had in the fridge. Here I've mixed the noodles with minced beef, a green pepper, some shiitake mushrooms and a few store-cupboard ingredients. Hope you enjoy it!

PREP TIME: 10 minutes • **COOK IN:** 10 minutes • **SERVES:** 2–4 to share

200g (7oz) dried white shi wheat-flour noodles or medium egg noodles

1 tbsp of toasted sesame oil

1 tbsp of groundnut oil

2 cloves of garlic, crushed and finely chopped

400g (14oz) minced beef

1 tbsp of Shaohsing rice wine or dry sherry

1 green pepper, deseeded and diced

5 shiitake mushrooms, diced

1 x 400g tin of chopped tomatoes

1 tbsp of light soy sauce

1 tbsp of chilli oil

Pinch of sea salt

Pinch of ground white pepper

Handful of chopped coriander, plus a few sprigs to garnish

1 spring onion, finely sliced, to garnish

1. Cook the noodles in a saucepan of boiling water for 2–3 minutes until al dente, or according to the instructions on the packet. Drain, then rinse under cold running water and drain again. Drizzle with the toasted sesame oil and toss together to prevent the noodles from sticking to each other.

2. Heat a wok over a high heat until it starts to smoke and add the groundnut oil. Add the garlic and stir-fry a few seconds, then add the minced beef. Break the beef up in the wok, and as it starts to turn brown, pour in the rice wine or dry sherry.

3. Add the green pepper and mushrooms and stir-fry for 1 minute. Add the tinned tomatoes and bring to the boil. Season with the soy sauce, chilli oil and salt and pepper and stir in the chopped coriander. Remove from the heat and serve ladled on top of the noodles, garnished with the spring onion and coriander sprigs.

Prawn and yellow bean chow mein with pak choy

Quick, tasty and nutritious, this makes a great midweek supper. The yellow bean paste is a great store-cupboard ingredient, perfect for marinades and speedy home-cooked meals like this one.

PREP TIME: 5 minutes • **COOK IN:** 7 minutes • **SERVES:** 2

100g (3⅓oz) medium egg noodles

2 tbsps of toasted sesame oil

1 tbsp of groundnut oil

1 large clove of garlic, crushed and finely chopped

1 red chilli, deseeded and finely chopped

200g (7oz) cooked shelled and deveined tiger prawns

100g (3½oz) baby pak choy leaves

FOR THE SAUCE

1 tbsp of yellow bean paste

1 tbsp of light soy sauce

1 tbsp of Shaohsing rice wine or dry sherry

1 tbsp of cornflour

1. Cook the noodles in a saucepan of boiling water for 2–3 minutes until al dente, or according to the instructions on the packet. Drain, then rinse under cold running water and drain again. Drizzle the drained noodles with half the toasted sesame oil and toss together to prevent them from sticking to each other.

2. Meanwhile, mix together all the ingredients for the sauce, along with 100ml (3½fl oz) of water, and set aside.

3. Heat a wok over a high heat until it starts to smoke and then add the groundnut oil. Add the garlic and stir-fry for a few seconds, then add the chilli and fry for a few seconds more.

4. Add the prawns, pak choy and the sauce, then bring to the boil. Tip in the cooked noodles and toss together, then drizzle with the remaining toasted sesame oil and serve immediately.

> **ALSO TRY**
> For a vegetarian version of this dish, substitute the prawns with sliced deep-fried dofu or shiitake mushrooms.

Crayfish sweet chilli noodles

This is another of my favourite noodle salads, a dish that I made for one of my customers when I was running my food business. Herby, tangy, sweet and spicy, this recipe is healthy and nutritious too.

PREP TIME: 15 minutes, plus 30 minutes for chilling • **COOK IN:** 3 minutes • **SERVES:** 2

200g (7oz) dried yellow shi wheat-flour noodles or medium egg noodles

1 tbsp of toasted sesame oil

60g (2½oz) mixed leaves (such as watercress, rocket and baby spinach)

8 mangetout, finely sliced lengthways

2 spring onions, finely sliced

½ red pepper, deseeded and finely sliced

10 sprigs of mint

Small handful of coriander

100g (3½oz) cooked crayfish tails in brine, drained

Lime wedges, to serve (optional)

FOR THE DRESSING

Juice of ½ pink grapefruit (including 'bits')

2 tbsps of sweet chilli sauce

1 tbsp of extra-virgin olive oil

1 spring onion, finely chopped

Small handful of coriander, finely chopped, plus extra to garnish

1. Cook the noodles in a saucepan of boiling water for 2–3 minutes until al dente, or according to the instructions on the packet. Drain, then rinse under cold running water and drain again. Drizzle with the toasted sesame oil and toss together to prevent the noodles from sticking to each other. Transfer to a bowl, cover with cling film and place in the fridge to chill for 20 minutes.

2. Toss the chilled noodles with the remaining salad ingredients. Divide between two bowls, then cover with cling film and place in the fridge to chill for a further 10 minutes.

3. Just before serving, mix together the ingredients for the dressing, then pour over the salad, garnish with coriander and serve immediately with the lemon wedges (if using).

Dessert

W hen I was little and growing up in Taiwan, the only sweet treats my brother and I had to look forward to was Yakult or *nian gao* ('sticky cake') at Chinese New Year. We didn't have any sweets or puddings otherwise. Dessert was usually in the form of sweetened soups like red bean soup, green bean soup with ginger and rock sugar or *pai mu er* (white ear fungus soup with lotus nuts). Occasionally, we were treated to ice lollies by our great-grandfather, who had a sweet tooth and would buy them for us. The flavours were nothing like those you would find in a Western shop, however. They would include sweetcorn, red kidney bean, green mung bean, black sesame, peanut and taro – in fact, most of them were made from seeds or vegetables. But they were delicious. Whenever I return to Taiwan, I always hunt these out because they remind me so much of my childhood. I once had such a craving for them, I even made red kidney bean and vanilla ice cream and, although I say so myself, it was rather good. I urge you to try it sometime.

It was not until my family moved to South Africa that I encountered 'proper' sweets and desserts. At school we had little plastic tubs of Nutella – I thought I had died and gone to heaven when I first tried one! Then there was the toffee-coated popcorn and sponge pudding …

Although I was exposed to sweet dishes at school, they never featured on the menu at home. My mother would always make sure we had a plate or small bowl of fruit after dinner and it was the closest we got to dessert. Hence growing up I was always more of a 'savoury' than 'sweet' person.

It all changed when I first arrived in London. I remember taking a rather challenging exam, and before I knew it, I had been accepted to Mount School in North London. I was only 11 and things seemed very strange and new to me. Everyone kept asking if I was from Australia. I didn't know where Australia was – it was as foreign to me as my South African accent was to my schoolmates. Everyone said 'Yeah' and I said 'Jah'. At the Mount, I was exposed to English food, English comfort food. I remember my first apple crumble with custard – it was so good, I nearly licked the bowl clean! At first, I brought packed lunches to school, but after a few weeks I looked forward to school lunch with a passion, and it was the dessert menu that I had my eye on.

Desserts would consist of apple pie, rhubarb crumble, spotted dick, sticky toffee pudding, chocolate pudding, bread and butter pudding, treacle pudding, jam roly poly, trifle and Eton mess … I was in heaven. I couldn't understand why all the other girls hated school dinners so much. (I suspected it was more to do with trying to look cool.)

We didn't study home economics at school, but I did learn a little about French cooking. Our French teacher went by the name of Madame Wheeler and she was quite a character and rather hot-tempered. Luckily, I always did as I was told so I was mostly in her good books. Other girls were not so lucky, like Emily – poor Emily. Madame Wheeler would go around the classroom asking us questions individually. If you got the answer wrong or mispronounced a word, she would quickly lose patience. One day she was so incensed by Emily's failure to pronounce a word properly that she shrieked at her: 'It's DEEEEEmanche, Emiiiily, DEEEEEEmanche!!!' I can remember very few words in French, but I'll never forget that one! Anyway, one week Madame Wheeler gave us an assignment to bake a French dessert called clafoutis. She wanted to immerse us in French culture. So we all went home and cooked our own version of the dish and brought it to school. It was a great recipe – the dark, sweet, slightly sour cherries were so delicious – and the best lesson I had ever had. After that, Madame Wheeler became my favourite teacher – I thought she was God!

I enjoy eating desserts more than I do cooking them, I have to admit. When I entertain, I cook Chinese and I like to go to town on the savoury dishes, but when it comes to dessert, I usually knock up something quick and simple. It's not just to do with personal preference, however. Because Chinese dishes can be quite strong in flavour, I like to counterbalance them with something light and refreshing. These desserts are by no means the only ones in my repertoire, but I prefer to rely on recipes that don't take long to make or can be prepared in advance to save stress and give me more time with my guests.

Takeaways don't normally feature desserts and so I have taken a bit of creative licence here, although they would certainly feature on the menu of my fantasy takeaway. I would serve tubs of homemade ice cream, like the Mango Ice Cream included here (see page 217), in addition to my Banana Toffee Fritters and Plum, Apple and Lychee Spring Rolls in Cinnamon Sugar (see pages 215 and 212. At Chinese New Year, I would serve my customers slices of celebratory *Nian Gao* (see page 220) with small tubs of crème caramel or sticky toffee dipping sauce. The possibilities are endless!

Mango and coconut pudding with orange cinnamon syrup

I love mango pudding – it makes the perfect summer dessert. If you find yourself craving this when mangoes aren't in season and therefore not at their best, just use tinned ones instead.

PREP TIME: 10 minutes, plus 1 hour for chilling/setting • **COOK IN:** 3 minutes • **SERVES:** 4

425g (15oz) fresh mangoes or tinned mangoes plus syrup

450ml (16fl oz) tinned coconut milk

100g (3½oz) caster sugar

1 x 20g packet of leaf gelatine, soaked in water and then squeezed

FOR THE ORANGE CINNAMON SYRUP

50ml (2fl oz) golden syrup

50ml (2fl oz) freshly squeezed orange juice

Juice of ½ lemon

1 star anise

TO SERVE

12 raspberries

4 sprigs of mint

1 small bowl of crushed pistachio nuts (optional)

1. Purée the mango (including the syrup if using tinned mangoes) in a blender. Transfer to a bowl and add the coconut milk and sugar, then mix well to dissolve the sugar.

2. In a measuring jug, measure 50ml (2fl oz) of hot water and add the soaked gelatine. Stir well to dissolve, then add to the mango and coconut purée and mix well.

3. Ladle the mixture into individual dishes, then place on a tray, cover with cling film and leave in the fridge for at least 1 hour to chill and set.

4. Meanwhile, to make the orange cinnamon syrup, place all the ingredients in a small saucepan and bring to the boil to infuse the flavours. Stir well and then set aside to cool to room temperature before covering and transferring to the fridge to chill for 20 minutes.

5. When ready to serve, pour 2 tbsps of the syrup over each pudding, decorate each with 3 raspberries and a sprig of mint and allow your guests to sprinkle some crushed pistachio nuts over the top.

Plum, apple and lychee spring rolls in cinnamon sugar

This is a delicious late summer/early autumn dessert. Tart apples, juicy soft plums and sweet lychees are fried in butter, cinnamon and sugar and then wrapped in pastry and fried until crisp. They are delicious served with a scoop of vanilla ice cream.

PREP TIME: 15 minutes, plus 30 minutes for cooling
COOK IN: 5 minutes • **MAKES:** 12 small spring rolls

60g (2½oz) unsalted butter

1 dessert apple, peeled and cored then cut into 5mm (¼in) cubes

50g (2oz) ripe plums, stones removed, chopped into 5mm (¼in) cubes

1 tsp of granulated sugar

1 tsp of ground cinnamon

50g (2oz) fresh lychees, peeled and stones removed, or tinned lychees, chopped into 5mm (¼in) cubes

12 spring-roll wrappers (14.5cm/6in square)

1 tbsp of cornflour mixed with 1 tbsp of hot water

20g (¾oz) caster sugar

Vanilla ice cream, to serve

TO DECORATE

12 strawberries, stalks left on

4 sprigs of mint

1. Heat a wok over a medium heat and melt half the butter. Add the apple and plums and stir-fry for a few minutes until slightly softened. Add the granulated sugar and half the cinnamon and fry until the apples are crisp, then stir in the lychees. Remove from the heat and allow the mixture to cool. (The filling can be made in advance, if you prefer.)

2. Take a spring-roll wrapper and place it with one of the corners facing you so that the square forms a diamond. Place 1 tbsp of the fruit filling in the centre of the pastry, then brush each corner with some of the cornflour paste.

3. Bring together the two side corners of the 'diamond' so that they meet over the filling, then bring the bottom corner up over the filling and continue rolling up to the top corner. Dab the top corner with more cornflour paste and press lightly to secure the spring roll. Continue filling the remaining wrappers until you have made 12 in total.

4. Heat a wok over a medium heat and melt the remaining butter. Place the spring rolls in the pan and fry for 1 minute or until golden.

5. Place the caster sugar and remaining cinnamon on a plate and carefully roll the spring rolls in the mixture. Decorate with the strawberries and sprigs of mint and serve with a scoop of vanilla ice cream.

Banana toffee fritters

I first had this in a Chinese restaurant here in the UK. It is a classic, my favourite Chinese dessert, and some restaurants will use a combination of apples and bananas. This is just as delicious with tinned Jackfruit for a Southeast Asian twist, but bananas are my favourite.

PREP TIME: 10 minutes • **COOK IN:** 10 minutes • **SERVES:** 4 to share

600ml (1 pint) groundnut oil
3 ripe bananas, plus 1 extra
  banana, sliced, to serve
125g (4½oz) demerara sugar
2 tbsps of white sesame seeds
Vanilla ice cream, to serve

FOR THE BATTER
125g (4½oz) self-raising flour
2 eggs, beaten
Pinch of salt

> **CHING'S TIP**
> Take care not to overheat the sugar or it will taste burned, so keep the heat on medium-low when you are making the toffee coating for the fritters.

1. First make the batter for the fritters. Sift the flour into a bowl and stir in the beaten eggs, then gradually add 2 tbsps of water and mix together into a batter. Add the salt and leave to stand for a few minutes.

2. Place a wok over a high heat and add the groundnut oil. Heat the oil to 180°C (350°F) or until a cube of bread dropped in turns golden brown in 15 seconds and floats to the surface.

3. Peel the bananas, removing any 'strings' from the fruit, and break each one into about 4 pieces. Dip the banana pieces one by one into the batter and then add to the hot oil. Fry for 3–4 minutes or until the pieces turn golden and float to the surface of the oil, then carefully remove from the oil with a slotted spoon and drain on kitchen paper.

4. While the banana fritters are draining, heat a small wok or frying pan over a medium heat and add the sugar. As the sugar starts to turn to liquid, quickly add the fritters and coat well in the caramelised sugar. Sprinkle over the sesame seeds as you turn the fritters in the pan: they will become toasted as they hit the hot sugar.

5. Remove the toffee fritters from the pan and dip them quickly in a bowl of iced water, then place on individual plates. Decorate with the banana slices and serve with a scoop of vanilla ice cream.

Pineapple and mango crunch trifle

My friends Lina and Alex came round one Sunday for lunch. I'd been dying to make them a special Chinese meal but had stayed up late the night before watching *Lawrence of Arabia* and then slept in, with no time to head to the supermarket. I had pretty much got all the ingredients for lunch in my fridge except for dessert, so I had to improvise with whatever came to hand. Hunting around, I located a packet of Fox's Golden Crunch Creams, a pineapple, half a mango, some double cream and a tin of custard and, hey presto, this summery pudding was born (and it wasn't too bad either!).

PREP TIME: 10 minutes • **SERVES:** 4

10 crunchy sandwich vanilla-cream biscuits, roughly chopped

200g (7oz) peeled pineapple, cut into 1cm (½in) cubes

200g (7oz) peeled mango, cut into 1cm (½in) cubes

Seeds from ½ pomegranate (optional)

4 tsps of Grand Marnier or pineapple or mango juice

200ml (7fl oz) shop-bought fresh custard

100ml (3½fl oz) double cream

Handful of raspberries, slices of strawberry or pomegranate seeds, to decorate (optional)

FOUR SMALL TUMBLERS (ABOUT 250ML/9FL OZ IN VOLUME)

1. Roughly chop up the biscuits and divide between the four tumblers.

2. Arrange the fruit in layers in the glasses, then drizzle over the Grand Marnier or fruit juice and top each tumbler with a layer of custard. Whip the cream into soft peaks and spoon on top of the custard.

3. Decorate with raspberries, slices of strawberry or a scattering of pomegranate seeds and serve.

Mango ice cream with exotic fruit

I love ice cream – but my favourite flavour is mango. This dessert can be prepared in advance and complements most savoury dishes. It's cleansing and refreshing and perfect for a hot summer's day.

PREP TIME: 10 minutes, plus 1–7 hours for cooling/freezing
COOK IN: 2 minutes • **SERVES:** 4

2 large mangoes, peeled and stones removed, then sliced

900ml (1 pint 12fl oz) double cream

90g (3¼oz) caster sugar

TO SERVE

2 mangoes, peeled and stones removed, then sliced

12 fresh lychees, peeled and stones removed, or tinned lychees, sliced

4 large strawberries, hulled and sliced

Seeds of ½ pomegranate

1. Place the mangoes in a blender and whiz to a purée, then set aside.

2. Pour the double cream into a large saucepan placed over a low heat and add the caster sugar and the puréed mangoes. Mix well and then remove from the heat and set aside to cool. Once cooled, pour into an ice-cream machine and follow the instructions for making the ice cream.

3. To make the ice cream by hand, transfer the mixture to a freezer-proof container, cover and place in the freezer for 2–3 hours or until just frozen. Remove from the freezer and, using a fork or whisk, break up any ice crystals. Return to the freezer for a further 2 hours, break up the ice again, then refreeze until solid. Just before serving, transfer the ice cream to the fridge to allow it to soften a little.

4. To serve, divide the sliced mango between individual dessert bowls. Add 2–3 scoops of the mango ice cream, then decorate with the lychee and strawberry slices and scatter over the pomegranate seeds.

Zesty fruit salad with star anise syrup

In the Chinese home, we mostly have a plate of fruit for dessert. On special occasions my father would go to a Chinese supermarket and bring back a large pomelo or Chinese grapefruit. Almost double the size of a Western grapefruit, this has a thick, pale green skin and opaque flesh. It's also less juicy than a Western grapefruit, which allows you to peel and segment the fruit more easily. My father would peel the pomelo in one piece so that my brother and I could pop it on our heads like a helmet! I like to serve this at Chinese New Year, with the orange segments signifying gold (or wealth) and the reddish colour of the pomegranate seeds signifying good luck. Delicious and refreshing, with a hint of spice in the syrup, this makes a perfect dessert to follow a rich main course.

PREP TIME: 15 minutes, plus 20 minutes for chilling • **COOK IN:** 2 minutes • **SERVES:** 2

1 large pink grapefruit, peeled and segmented

2 small oranges, peeled and segmented

½ pomelo or 1 pink grapefruit, peeled and segmented

6 lychees, peeled and stones removed, or tinned lychees

Seeds from ½ large pomegranate

FOR THE STAR ANISE SYRUP

50ml (2fl oz) golden syrup

50ml (2fl oz) freshly squeezed orange juice

2 star anise

¼ tsp of ground cinnamon

1. Mix together all the citrus fruit in a large bowl, cover with cling film and leave to chill in the fridge for 20 minutes.

2. Meanwhile, place all the ingredients for the syrup in a wok or saucepan and warm through over a low heat, mixing well to combine and allow the different flavours to infuse. Remove from the heat and allow to cool, then cover and chill in the fridge for 20 minutes.

3. Just before serving, add the lychees to the citrus fruit, then divide the fruit between shallow dessert bowls. Drizzle over the chilled syrup and sprinkle over the pomegranate seeds, then serve immediately.

Nian gao

Nian gao, or 'sticky cake', is traditionally served at Chinese New Year as a symbol of togetherness among families. *Nian* ('sticky') also means 'year', while *gao* ('cake') can mean 'high', to convey the sense that you rise 'higher' each year. This is matched by the New Year saying '*Nian nian sheng gao*' ('Every year you rise in the ranks'), to indicate progress in your studies or career.

Nian gao consists of a sweetened dough made with glutinous rice flour. It is steamed and then left to cool and set. It's then dipped in batter and fried until the outside is crisp and inside the cake has melted to a 'sticky' consistency, like marshmallow but denser. It is utterly delicious, and although the cake takes a bit of time to cook, it's very simple to make and you can prepare it in advance. My grandmother would cook it for us back in Taiwan, sometimes adding red beans or red Chinese dates to the cake mixture. This is my version of the dish, to which I've added just a hint of vanilla and a little wheat starch to make the dough less dense once it's cooked. Both glutinous rice flour and wheat starch can be bought from a Chinese supermarket.

PREP TIME: 10 minutes, plus 50 minutes for cooling/chilling
COOK IN: 65 minutes • **SERVES:** 4 to share

125g (4½oz) soft light brown sugar
150g (5oz) glutinous rice flour
30g (1¼oz) wheat starch
1 tsp of vanilla extract
Groundnut oil, for deep-frying

FOR THE BATTER
100g (3½oz) potato flour
1 egg, beaten
Pinch of salt

ONE 20CM (8IN) DIAMETER SANDWICH TIN WITH 3CM (1¼IN) SIDES

1. Fill a saucepan with 200ml (7fl oz) of water and bring to the boil. Remove from the heat, stir in the sugar until dissolved and set aside to cool.

2. Sift together the rice flour and wheat starch into a bowl, then pour in the cooled sugar syrup and mix well to form a dough.

3. Line the sandwich tin with foil and pour in the cake mixture. Place the tin in a bamboo steamer set over a saucepan of boiling water (making sure the bottom of the steamer doesn't touch the water) and steam on a high heat for 1 hour.

4. Remove the tin from the steamer and allow to cool to room temperature, then place in the fridge to chill and set for 30 minutes.

5. Just before serving, slice the cake into 2.5cm (1in) pieces. Next make the batter by mixing together the potato flour with the beaten egg, salt and 2 tbsps of water.

6. Place a wok over a high heat and half fill it with groundnut oil. Heat the oil to 180°C (350°F) or until a cube of bread dropped in turns golden brown in 15 seconds and floats to the surface.

7. Dip the cake pieces in the batter, then carefully lower into the hot oil and deep-fry for 5 minutes or until golden brown. Remove from the oil with a slotted spoon and drain on kitchen paper, then serve them hot on a plate so that everyone can help themselves.

Equipment

Woks

Buying and caring for your wok

There is nothing more traditional in Chinese cooking than using the wok. This great invention has been used for centuries to help feed millions of people all over the world. Woks come in various sizes and are made from different materials, so choosing one can be challenging. Traditional cast-iron woks are quite heavy and require seasoning, which is not too difficult. The wok comes coated with a film of oil; wash this off using a sponge and washing-up liquid, then dry the wok over a high flame on the stove. Next, add a little oil to the wok (sesame oil is good because it burns quickly) and then use kitchen paper to rub in the oil over the entire wok, giving it a darkened, blackened effect. Once your wok is seasoned, don't use a metal scourer or iron wool on it, as you will take off the seasoning.

For those who prefer a lighter wok, I would recommend one made from carbon steel, which you season in the same way as the cast-iron wok. If you are new to wok cooking or just short of time, buy a non-stick wok made from carbon steel – it will require less oil for cooking than a cast-iron one, so is healthier too.

When choosing your wok, make sure it feels comfortable and right for you. I prefer a one-handled wok with a medium handle that is not too thick to hold. In terms of size, choose a medium wok between 30cm (12in) and 40cm (16in) in diameter, which will hold a medium-sized bamboo steamer comfortably and allow you to cook enough to serve at least four.

For those who don't have a gas stove, I would say invest in a new cooker! I find that electric stoves are just not right for wok cooking – you can buy a flat-bottomed wok, but you never really get enough heat to cook the food. However, you could invest in a good electric wok, which I have used and found not too bad.

Techniques for cooking in a wok

Stir-frying

The classic use of a wok – a touch of oil and lots of stirring – ensures that the ingredients keep their crunch and take on a smoky flavour. To help you cook your dish to perfection, however, there are a few things to observe.

1. Preparation

Always prepare the ingredients before you start, as you won't have time once you start cooking. Cut all the meat or fish to the same size – this ensures that the pieces cook in the same time. This principle also applies to vegetables. For leafy vegetables, cut them on the diagonal – this exposes them to more heat in the wok and they will cook more rapidly.

2. Choosing the right oil

Most oils with a high heating point can be used, such as sunflower, groundnut and vegetable oil, but avoid toasted sesame oil, as this has a low heating point and burns quickly – use it for seasoning your dishes. Olive oil isn't ideal because its flavour does not suit all Chinese dishes. It is best to use flavourless oil. My favourite is groundnut – it has a slight nutty aroma that is not strong enough to overpower a dish, but acts as a great base on which to build layers of flavour.

3. The correct heat

To prepare the wok for stir-frying, heat it to a high heat until it starts to smoke, then add the oil and swirl it around in the wok. During the cooking process, keep an eye on the flame and level of heat in the wok both before and after adding the food – the temperature in the wok will fall once the ingredients have been added, so you want the heat high enough to sear the food, but not so high that you burn the ingredients.

4. Adding raw ingredients and timing

The ingredients should go into the wok in the following order. Add the Chinese essentials such as garlic, ginger and chillies first. Secondly, add the meat or seafood, and then, lastly, the vegetables, with a sprinkling of water to create steam. This order of cooking helps to retain the bite of the vegetables. It is important to dry the ingredients before you add them to the wok or the oil will spit, and if there is too much moisture, the ingredients will stew rather than fry. If you are using sauces or meats marinated in sauces, don't add the sauce or marinade until the end of the stir-frying process to ensure it doesn't all evaporate, and to prevent the food from stewing.

Sometimes the meat/protein is cooked first and then removed from the wok while the vegetables are stir-fried. It is then returned to the wok for the final mixing with seasoning. I find that you don't always have to cook in this way (recipes vary). There are some dishes where you can add the meat/protein after the garlic, ginger and chillies and then, once they start to cook, you can add the rest of the ingredients; this helps to ensure that the meat/protein is not overly cooked. So timing is important in wok cooking – knowing when the ingredient is ready for seasoning and when to add other ingredients. Work with what is best for you.

5. Adding cooked ingredients

Cooked noodles or cooked rice can be added to the wok at the end of the cooking process and combined with the rest of the ingredients, together with all the seasoning.

Steaming

Food cooked in a bamboo steamer takes on a subtle bamboo fragrance. This technique is a wonderful way of preparing a healthy meal; it's fast and fun too. You can also serve your food in the steamer, with the lid on; this helps to keep the food warm for longer.

1. Making sure the wok is stable

If you have a gas stove, invest in a wok rest; this helps to keep the wok stable and secure.

2. Filling the wok with water

Fill the wok (or a saucepan) half full with water and place the bamboo steamer over the top, ensuring that the water doesn't touch the base of the steamer. Depending on the recipe, either place the food to be steamed directly in the steamer or on a heatproof plate. Put the lid on and steam. If necessary, top up the wok with more boiling water as the food cooks.

3. Size of the bamboo steamer

Bamboo steamers vary in size, so make sure you buy one that sits snugly across the wok and will not touch the water. If necessary, you can sit the steamer on a heatproof plate, bowl or rack in the wok to raise it above the water. For those who love to cook a feast, you can pile the steamers up as high as you want (although you will need a powerful flame that can produce enough steam to reach the highest steamer; I would say two or three piled high should be okay).

4. A final tip

Before you attempt to remove the lid of the steamer, make sure you always turn the flame off. I have been impatient many times and have burned my hands and arms from the hot steam.

Note: If you don't have a large enough bamboo steamer for the ingredient you want to cook (such as a large fish), place the food on a heatproof plate and put on a rack in a roasting tin. Carefully pour boiling water into the tin, then cover with foil and place in the oven. Cook for the time stated in the recipe at 200°C (400°F), gas mark 6.

Deep-frying

You might think this not a very healthy way of cooking, but if the oil is hot enough, once the food is dropped in it will cook at such a high temperature that the outside edges are almost 'sealed', not allowing the ingredient to absorb any more oil, and the high heat continues to cook the inside of the food.

1. Making sure the wok is stable
If you are cooking on a gas stove, invest in a wok rest; this helps to keep the wok stable and secure – very important when deep-frying.

2. Making sure the oil is hot enough

To get the best results, use a deep-frying thermometer and follow the temperature stated in the recipe. If the oil is too cold, the food will take longer to cook and be too oily. If the temperature is too hot, the food will burn and be undercooked on the inside. If you don't have a thermometer, then you can use the 'bread test', which I refer to in my recipes. Be particularly careful when deep-frying in a wok – don't overfill it, or leave it unattended.

3. Adding and removing the food

When lowering food into deep oil, I use a utensil called a 'spider'. It is a web-like, woven steel mesh scooper that works well as a strainer. Use it also for lifting fried foods from the wok (draining much oil in the process) on to dishes lined with kitchen paper (again, to help drain excess oil). The 'spider' comes in different sizes and you should be able to find it in all good Chinese supermarkets and kitchen/cookware shops. They often have a handle made of bamboo. Alternatively, you can use a slotted spoon or tongs, depending on the type of food being cooked.

4. Golden rules when deep-frying
• Make sure the wok is stable, or use a wok stand.
• Don't overfill the wok with oil – it should be no more than half full, so there is less chance of bubbling and spilling over.
• Make sure the food is dry, as this prevents spitting.
• For best results, never re-use oil.
• Use a large, long pair of bamboo chopsticks or metal tongs to help you turn food over if necessary (not plastic chopsticks, as they melt).
• Serve fried food immediately, as it will start to lose its crunch and crispness. However, if unavoidable, keep the food hot in a preheated oven before serving.

Other cooking utensils

The following would also be useful to have in the kitchen:

Wok cover

Invest in a wok cover; this will allow you to stew, steam, boil and smoke food using your wok. It should have a handle on top and fit snugly and firmly on the wok.

Wok brush

This is a wooden brush with long hard bristles that is used with hot water to clean the wok. It's not essential, but can take the hard work out of cleaning.

Chinese spatula/wooden spoon

Traditionally, a metal spatula is used to allow you to manoeuvre the food and scoop it out of the wok. This is fine for seasoned woks, but you may end up scratching off the non-stick coating if you use a non-stick wok. I would suggest a wooden spoon as an alternative.

Ladle

A Chinese ladle is small and bowl-shaped to allow you to scoop up soups and sauces from the wok, but I also use a normal ladle. Try to find one made from stainless steel, as carbon steel can rust easily.

Chinese cleaver/good knife

It is essential to invest in a good knife. I tend to use a medium-sized stainless-steel chef's knife made from one continuous piece of metal. However, I also have a stainless-steel Chinese cleaver with a wooden handle. Cleavers are particularly useful for hacking meat with bones and are also handy for slicing, shredding, dicing, mincing and mashing (by using the side of the blade against the chopping board). Of course, you can use a food processor instead, but I find it is good therapy to chop away with the cleaver.

Cutting board

Choose a solid, large wooden chopping board and make sure you clean it well after use. I keep three different boards: one for meat, one for seafood and one for fruit and vegetables.

Glossary

Unless otherwise stated, the ingredients should be available in most high-street supermarkets.

Angelica sinensis (herb/dried)
Commonly known as Chinese angelica or dong quai, *Angelica sinensis* is grown in China and is widely used in Traditional Chinese Medicine to strengthen the blood and treat gynaecological problems. All parts of the plant are used in cooking, including the leaves, stem and roots. Dried pieces of the root are used in herbal soups, providing a strong woody aroma when cooked. Available from Chinese supermarkets.

Bamboo shoots (tinned)
Drain tinned bamboo shoots and use them in stir-fries and soups. They are rarely available fresh.

Basmati rice (dried)
Grown in India and Pakistan, basmati has a delicate, aromatic flavour. Being longer-grained than jasmine rice, it is less sticky when freshly cooked and so works well in fried-rice dishes. It is available as both white and brown rice. Both types can be used for a stir-fry, but for salads I prefer the brown variety, as it has more of a bite.

Black beans – *see* Fermented salted black beans

Black rice (dried)
Black rice – or 'forbidden rice', as it is sometimes known, because in former times only the Chinese emperor was allowed to eat it – is particularly rich in iron and antioxidants (its colour being due to its high anthocyanin content). The rice is also ground to a fine powder to make black rice noodles. It has a deep nutty taste and is delicious in rice salads, adding texture and flavour as well as a striking contrast in colour. Sometimes available from Western supermarkets, it can also be found in a good Chinese supermarket.

Black rice vinegar – *see* Chinkiang black rice vinegar

Cassia bark – *see* Cinnamon stick/bark

Century eggs (preserved)
These are duck eggs (sometimes called thousand-year-old eggs) that have been buried in salt, tea leaves and rice husk, covered with sodium bicarbonate and left to mature for 40–50 days. The yolk has a rich creamy texture and, when served chilled, the white is clear, jelly-like and fragrant. Do not confuse these with preserved salted duck eggs – matured for 20 days, they have a deep orange yolk and an opaque, clean white.

Chilli bean paste (sauce)
Mainly used in Sichuan cooking, this is made from broad beans and chillies that have been fermented with salt to give a deep brown-red sauce. Some versions include fermented soya beans or garlic. This makes a great stewing sauce, but use with caution, as some varieties are extremely hot.

Chilli oil (oil)
This is made from dried red chillies heated in oil to give a spicy orange-red fiery oil. Some chilli oils also contain specks of dried chillies. Available from any Chinese supermarket or you can make your own: heat a wok over a medium heat and add some groundnut oil. Add dried chilli flakes with seeds and heat for 2 minutes. Take off the heat and leave to infuse in the oil until the oil has completely cooled. Decant into a glass jar with a tight lid and store for a month before using. For a clear oil, pass through a sieve.

Chilli sauce (ingredient/dipping sauce)
This can be used in cooking or as a dipping sauce. There are several varieties; some are flavoured with vinegar and garlic, such as Guilin chilli sauce. For sweet chilli sauce I use the Mae Ploy brand.

Chinese five spice/Chinese five-spice powder (spice)
This is a blend of cinnamon, cloves, Sichuan peppercorns, fennel and star anise. These five spices give the sour, bitter, pungent, sweet and salty flavours in Chinese cooking. The powdered form is great for marinades and when you want the flavours to be wholly incorporated into a dish. The whole spices can be crushed and used as a rub on meats as well as for flavouring oils.

Chinese wood ear mushrooms (dried)
These dark brown-black fungi have ear-shaped caps and are very crunchy in texture. They do not impart flavour, but add colour and crispness to any dish. They should be soaked in hot

water for 20 minutes before cooking – they will double in size. After soaking they should be rinsed well to remove any dirt. Store the dried pieces in a glass jar and seal tightly. Available from Chinese supermarkets.

Chinkiang black rice vinegar (condiment)

Made from fermented rice, this strong aromatic vinegar comes from Jiangsu province, where it is produced in the capital, Nanjing. The taste is mellow and earthy and gives dishes a wonderful smoky flavour. Balsamic vinegar makes a good substitute. Available from Chinese supermarkets.

Choy sum (fresh)

Closely related to pak choy, choy sum is a vegetable grown for its tender crunchy stalks and flavoursome leaves, which are used in a whole range of dishes, especially soups and stir-fries. Available from Chinese supermarkets.

Cinnamon stick/bark (spice)

This is the dried bark of various trees of the *Cinnamomum* genus, one of the more common being the cassia tree. It can be used in whole pieces or ground and is one of the components of Chinese five spice. 'True' cinnamon, also known as Ceylon cinnamon, adds a sweet woody fragrance to any dish. Cassia bark is similar but has a woodier aroma; less expensive than cinnamon, it is more widely available and often sold in ground form as 'cinnamon'. Cinnamon is also said to have health-giving properties, such as preventing the common cold and aiding digestion.

Cloves (spice)

The clove tree is an evergreen and its dried flower buds are the aromatic spice that is one of the components of Chinese five spice. Cloves are strong and quite pungent in flavour. They are also used in Traditional Chinese Medicine to help digestion and promote the healthy function of the stomach, spleen and kidneys.

Congee (dish)

A type of plain soupy rice or rice porridge. Can be combined with scrambled eggs, pickled turnip, salted peanuts, fermented bean curd (dofu ru), pickled cucumbers and bamboo shoots pickled in chilli oil.

Coriander (herb/fresh)

This is mainly used as a garnish or in soups, stir-fries, stews and cold tossed salads. Both the leaves and stems of the herb are used.

Coriander seeds (spice)

The dried seeds of the coriander herb. When ground, they give a distinctive warm citrusy aroma to sweet and savoury dishes.

Cumin (spice)

This is the dried seed of the herb *Cuminum cyminum*, and belongs to the parsley family. When ground the spice has a distinctive, slightly bitter but warm flavour.

Curry powder (spice)

There are many different blends of curry powder. As well as Chinese five-spice powder, some curry powders also include coriander, turmeric, cumin, ginger and garlic.

Daikon or white radish (fresh)

This grows in the ground like a root vegetable, and resembles a large white carrot. It has a peppery and crunchy taste and can be eaten raw, pickled or cooked. Daikon contains vitamin C and diastase, an enzyme that helps digestion. It can be sliced or shredded and added to soups, salads and stir-fries. The Koreans use this vegetable to make kimchi, their famous pickle. Store in a sealed bag – daikon has a pungent smell.

Dark soy sauce (condiment)

Made from wheat and fermented soya beans, dark soy sauce has been aged a lot longer than the light soy variety. It is mellower and less salty in taste than light soy, and is used to give flavour and colour.

Deep-fried dofu (bean curd) (fresh)

This is fresh bean curd that has been deep-fried to a golden brown to make it crispy and crunchy on the outside. Usually found in the chilled sections of Chinese supermarkets.

Dofu – *see* Fresh bean curd

Dofu ru – *see* Fermented bean curd

Dried chilli flakes (spice)

These are made from dried whole red chillies, including the seeds, which are crushed into flakes – they give a fiery heat when added to dishes.

Dried Chinese mushrooms (dried)

These have a strong aroma and need to be soaked in hot water for 20 minutes before cooking. They have a slightly salty taste and complement savoury dishes well. After soaking, the stem can be left on or discarded. They are available from Chinese supermarkets. You can use dried shiitake or porcini mushrooms as a substitute.

Dried shrimps (dried)

These are shrimps that have been pre-cooked and then dried and salted to preserve them. To use, soak them in hot water for 20 minutes to soften them, then drain. Orange-red in colour and very pungent in aroma and taste, they come in packets. As with all preserved ingredients, it is best to store them in an airtight container. Available from Chinese supermarkets.

Egg noodles (fresh/dried)

The most common type of noodle, they are made from egg yolk, wheat flour and salt and come in various thicknesses and shapes. Some are flat and thin, others are long and rounded like spaghetti; some are flat and coiled in a ball. Available in various dried and fresh varieties. Store the fresh variety in the fridge for up to five days.

Enoki mushrooms (fresh)

These are tiny, white, very thin, long-stemmed mushrooms with a mild delicate flavour. When raw, they give great texture to salads. When lightly steamed, they are slightly chewy. They require very little cooking.

Fennel seeds (spice)

Fennel is a strong aromatic spice that has a slight aniseed aroma and flavour, but is much sweeter. It is one of the ingredients in Chinese five spice. Delicious when toasted or pan-fried and added to dishes.

Fermented bean curd (dofu ru) (preserved)

This is bean curd that has been preserved and flavoured with chilli, salt and spices. It is often cubed, comes in many flavours and white and red varieties are available. It is quite strong in flavour and is eaten on its own or used as a marinade, condiment or an accompaniment to congee. Found in glass jars in Chinese supermarkets.

Fermented salted black beans (dried)

These are small black soya beans that have been preserved in salt and so they must be rinsed in cold water before use. A common ingredient, they are used to make black bean sauce and can be found in Chinese supermarkets. Only substitute with black bean sauce if you can buy a very good-quality one, otherwise the dish won't taste the same.

Fish floss (dried)

Prepared in a similar way to pork floss, this is a form of dried shredded fish that is used as a topping for many savoury dishes. Available from Chinese supermarkets.

Fish sauce (nam pla) (condiment)

Made from fermented fish, this is a staple ingredient in Southeast Asian cooking for curries, soups and sauces.

Five spice/Five-spice powder

– see Chinese five spice/Chinese five-spice powder

Fresh bean curd (dofu) (fresh)

Described as the 'cheese' of China, fresh bean curd is made from protein-rich soya bean curd. It is white and quite bland, but takes on the flavour of whatever ingredients it is cooked with. It is used as a meat substitute in a vegetarian diet. In Japan it is called tofu and in Chinese, dofu. The texture is quite creamy and silky and there are various varieties, such as firm, soft and silken. The firm variety is great in soups, salads and stir-fries. Silken has a cream cheese-like texture. Dofu is protein-rich and contains B vitamins, isoflavones and calcium. The fresh variety is usually found in the chilled sections of Chinese supermarkets and can be kept chilled in the fridge for up to one week.

Garam masala (spice)

This is a blend of ground spices ('masala' meaning 'spice'), varying in its composition, but often including the spices that make up Chinese five spice. It is used widely in Indian cuisine and other South Asian dishes.

Glutinous rice (dried)

Grown throughout South Asia, this is a type of short-grain rice that is especially sticky (hence 'glutinous' or 'glue-like') when cooked. Available from Chinese supermarkets, it is used mainly in desserts.

Glutinous rice flour (ingredient)

Milled from glutinous rice, this is used in baking and as a thickener. Available from Chinese supermarkets.

Goji berries (dried)

Also known as wolfberries, these belong to the Solanaceae plant family (which includes potatoes, peppers and tomatoes) and are native to southeastern Europe and Asia. Rich in antioxidants, they are used in Traditional Chinese Medicine to boost the immune system and improve blood circulation, among other applications. The dried berries, which have a sweet, liquorice-like flavour, are added to herbal soups and congee, and brewed as a tea. (See also Matrimony vine.)

Groundnut oil (oil)

This pale oil is extracted from peanuts and has a subtle, nutty flavour. It can be heated to high temperatures without burning and is great to use in a salad dressing. As an alternative, use vegetable oil.

Hoisin sauce (sauce)

This is made from fermented soya beans, sugar, vinegar, star anise, sesame oil and red rice (which gives it a slight red colour). This is great used as a marinade and also as a dipping sauce.

Jasmine rice (dried)

This is a long-grain white rice that originates from Thailand. The rice has a nutty jasmine-scented aroma and makes a delicious accompaniment to dishes. As with most rice, you will need to rinse it before cooking until the water runs clear in order to get rid of any excess starch. White and silky, when cooked this rice is soft, white and fluffy.

Kimchi (preserved)

This is a traditional side dish from Korea, written references to it going back 5,000 years. It consists of vegetables – such as cabbage, cucumber or radishes – fermented or pickled with a variety of seasonings. Available from Chinese supermarkets.

Light soy sauce (condiment)

Light soy sauce is used in China instead of salt. It is made from fermented soya beans and wheat. A versatile and staple ingredient, it can be used in soups, stir-fries and braised and stewed dishes. Wheat-free varieties, called tamari, are available for those with wheat intolerance, and there are also low-sodium varieties for those watching their sodium intake.

Ligusticum wallichii (herb/dried)

Commonly known as Sichuan lovage, the dried root of this plant is used in Traditional Chinese Medicine to improve blood circulation. It is often steeped in tea or added to herbal soups. Available from Chinese supermarkets.

Lily bulbs (dried)

Widely grown in China both for medicinal purposes and as a root vegetable, these are available mostly in dried form and therefore need to be pre-soaked in warm water for 20 minutes before cooking. Similar in texture to the potato but with a sweeter flavour, they are used in various dishes, including soups and stir-fries. Considered cooling or 'yin' in character, the bulbs are regarded as especially suitable for eating in the summer. Available from Chinese supermarkets.

Lychee (fresh/tinned)

Red or amber in colour, oval in shape and with a brittle skin, lychees are the fruit of an evergreen tree native to southern China. The translucent white or pinkish flesh is aromatic and has a distinctive flavour. In the centre is a largish seed. Available fresh or tinned.

Mantou (fresh/frozen)

A type of bun originating in northern China, where wheat rather than rice is grown as the staple food, mantou are made with wheat flour. Soft and fluffy in texture, they are steamed and used to accompany various dishes. They are available from the frozen section of Chinese supermarkets or can be bought fresh from Chinese bakeries.

Matrimony vine (herb/dried)

Also known as wolfberry (see Goji berries), the dried root is used in the same way medicinally as the dried fruit. It is used in herbal stews and soups with a variety of other herbs to boost the immune system. Available from Chinese supermarkets.

Miso paste (paste)

This is a thick paste made from fermenting rice, barley, soya beans, salt and a fungus called kojikin. It comes in many varieties depending on the types of grains used to ferment the paste. It is used in Japanese soups and stocks and is sweet, earthy, fruity and salty.

Momoya (paste)

Used mainly in Japanese cuisine, this is a paste made from edible seaweed mixed with soy sauce, sesame oil and seeds, mirin, red pepper and garlic. Available from Chinese supermarkets, it makes a tasty garnish for rice dishes.

Mung bean noodles (dried)

Made from the starch of green mung beans and water, these noodles come in various thicknesses. Vermicelli is the thinnest type. Soak in hot water for 5–6 minutes before cooking. If using in soups or deep-frying, no pre-soaking is necessary. They become translucent when cooked. Great in salads, stir-fries and soups, or even in spring rolls. Vermicelli rice noodles can be used as a substitute.

Oyster mushrooms (fresh)

These fungi are oyster-shaped, moist, hairless and fragrant, and come in different colours – white, yellow and grey. It is soft and chewy with a slight oyster taste – great in a stir-fry.

Oyster sauce (sauce)

This seasoning sauce made from oyster extract originated in the Canton province in China. It is used liberally on vegetable dishes and can be used as a marinade. A vegetarian variety, prepared from mushrooms, is also available. This is a very salty ingredient, so taste the dish before adding.

Pak choy (fresh)

This is a vegetable from southern China. The broad green leaves, which taper to white stalks, are crisp and crunchy. It can be boiled, steamed or stir-fried in dishes.

Panko breadcrumbs (ingredient)

Produced in Japan, and made from bread without crusts, these have a crisper texture than other breadcrumbs. They are available from Asian stores and from many large supermarkets.

Pickled bamboo shoots in chilli oil (preserved)

These are bamboo shoots that have been pickled in vinegar, salt and chilli oil. They are great when used to flavour soups and stir-fries. They can usually be found in glass jars in Chinese supermarkets.

Pickled soy lettuce stems (preserved)

These are the stems of baby lettuce leaves that have been sliced and pickled in a soy brine. They have a salty flavour and are delicious as an accompaniment for plain rice. They can also be chopped finely and used in stir-fries. Available from Chinese supermarkets.

Pork floss (dried)
Pork floss or *rousong* is a form of dried shredded meat used in China as a topping for a variety of dishes, including congee. Available from Chinese supermarkets.

Potato flour (ingredient)
Potatoes are steamed, dried and then ground to give this silky-smooth white flour. It gives wonderful crispness to ingredients when they are coated in it before being shallow- or deep-fried. It is gluten free. Sometimes called potato starch, it is available from Chinese supermarkets and some supermarkets. Cornflour can be used as a substitute.

Preserved mustard greens/ Pickled Chinese cabbage (preserved)
The roots and leaves of the mustard cabbage are preserved with plenty of chilli and salt. They are available in either jars, tins or packets from Chinese supermarkets.

Preserved salted plums (preserved)
Much drier than prunes, these are eaten as a snack in China as well as used to make toppings and drinks. They are available from Chinese supermarkets in a variety of flavours.

Red dates (dried)
Also known as jujubes, these are the fruit of a small deciduous tree of the buckthorn family. When mature, the fruit are purplish-black and wrinkled-looking, like a small date. They are used both in Traditional Chinese Medicine (to alleviate stress) and

Chinese cuisine – eaten as a snack or preserved and used in various dishes.

Rhizome of rehmannia (herb/ dried)
This is the dried root of a perennial herb, also known as the Chinese foxglove, used in Traditional Chinese Medicine to treat anaemia, dizziness and constipation. Sweetish in taste, the root is also added to herbal soups and tonic drinks. Available from Chinese supermarkets.

Rice vinegar (condiment)
Plain rice vinegar is a clear vinegar made from fermented rice. It is used in dressings and for pickling and is more common than black rice vinegar. Cider vinegar can be used as a substitute.

Sesame oil – *see* Toasted sesame oil

Sesame paste (paste)
This is made from crushed roasted white sesame seeds blended with toasted sesame oil to give a golden-brown paste, and is used with other sauces to help flavour dishes. If you cannot find this rich sesame paste, you can use tahini (the Middle Eastern equivalent) instead, but it is a lot lighter in flavour and so you will need to add more toasted sesame oil. Available from Chinese supermarkets.

Sesame seeds (ingredient)
These oil-rich seeds come from an annual plant, *Sesamum indicum*. They add a nutty taste and a delicate texture to many Asian dishes. Available in black, white/yellow and red varieties, as well as toasted and untoasted – although they taste better freshly toasted.

Shaohsing rice wine (condiment)
This is wine made from rice, millet and yeast, that has been aged for between three and five years. Rice wine takes the 'odour' or 'rawness' out of meats

and fish and gives a bittersweet finish. Dry sherry makes a good substitute.

Shi wheat-flour noodles (dried)
'*Shi*' means 'thin/fine'. The noodles are available in white and yellow varieties. The yellow variety has added colouring. They are great in soups, salads and stir-fries. Use medium egg noodles as a substitute. Available from Chinese supermarkets.

Shiitake mushrooms (fresh)
These large dark-brown mushrooms are umbrella-shaped fungi that are prized for their culinary and medicinal properties. They contain all eight essential amino acids in more significant proportions than soya beans, milk, meat and eggs, as well as vitamins A, B, B_{12}, C and D, niacin and minerals. They are a staple in China, Japan and other parts of Asia, and are a popular source of protein.

Shimeji mushrooms (fresh)
Originating in East Asia, 'shimeji' comprise a number of species. When cooked, they have a crunchy texture and nutty flavour that goes well in stir-fries, soups and stews. Available from Chinese supermarkets.

Sichuan chillies/dried chilli flakes
There are many different varieties of Sichuan chillies – a common type is a short, fat, bright red chilli that is hot and fragrant. They are usually sun-dried. You can grind the whole chillies using a pestle and mortar to give flakes.

Sichuan peppercorns (spice)
Known as *hua jiao* in Mandarin Chinese, or 'flower pepper', these are the outer pod of a tiny fruit. They are widely used all over China and especially in western China. They can be wok-roasted, cooked in oil to flavour the oil or mixed with salt as

a condiment. They have a pungent citrusy aroma.

Sichuan preserved vegetables – *see* Preserved mustard greens

Snake beans (fresh)
Snake beans or long beans are mostly grown in Asia. They are long, plump green beans, sometimes with a purple tinge to them, and since they are quite long, some varieties tend to twist. The fatter beans are more tender and sweet when cooked. This nutritious bean contains beta-carotene, vitamin C and phosphorus, and the Chinese use this plant to make tonics for ailing kidneys or to treat stomach problems. They make a great accompaniment to many dishes.

Spring roll wrappers/pastry (fresh)
Made from wheat flour and starch, these are used for wrapping foods such as spring rolls before deep-frying. Available in the frozen sections of Chinese supermarkets. If you can find the type made with coconut oil and salt, they can be eaten raw, filled with salad and with dressings. Filo pastry makes a good substitute.

Star anise (spice)
A staple ingredient in Chinese cooking, these are called *bajiao* or 'eight horns' in Chinese. They are the fruits of a small evergreen plant that grows in southwest China. Star anise has an aniseed flavour and is one of the ingredients found in Chinese five spice.

Toasted sesame oil (condiment)
Made from pressed and toasted white sesame seeds, this oil is used as a flavouring and is not suitable for use as a cooking oil, since it burns easily. The flavour is intense, so use sparingly.

Tofu – *see* Fresh bean curd

Turmeric (spice)
This is a tuberous rhizome of the ginger family. The rhizomes are first cooked for several hours and then dried before being ground into a powder, deep yellow in colour. Turmeric imparts a strong yellow colour to any dish and gives a slightly mustardy, peppery, earthy flavour. It also has medicinal properties and is used for its antiseptic properties for cuts and burns.

Udon noodles – *see* Wheat-flour flat udon noodles

Vermicelli mung bean noodles – *see* Mung bean noodles

Vermicelli rice noodles (dried)
Similar to vermicelli mung bean noodles, these come in many different widths and varieties. Soak in hot water for 5 minutes before cooking to soften. If using in salads, soak for 20 minutes. If using in a soup, add them dry. They turn opaque white when cooked. Great in soups, salads and stir-fries.

Water chestnuts (tinned)
Water chestnuts are the roots of an aquatic plant that grows in freshwater ponds, marshes and lakes, and in slow-moving rivers and streams. Unpeeled, they resemble a chestnut in shape and colouring. They have a firm, crunchy texture. Sometimes available vacuum-packed, they are mostly sold in tins.

Wheat-flour flat udon noodles (dried)
This is a thin, white wheat-flour noodle. Do not confuse these with the thick Japanese udon noodle. They are great in soups, salads and stir-fries.

Wheat-flour pancakes (fresh)
Made from wheat flour, water and salt and rolled into very thin discs, these are steamed before serving

and accompany Peking duck and other dishes. They can be found in the frozen or chilled sections of any Chinese supermarket.

Wheat starch (dried)
Obtained from wheat grain, this white silken powder is combined with hot water and used to make dumpling skins that turn from opaque white to translucent white once steamed.

Wonton wrappers (fresh/ frozen)
Made from egg, wheat flour, salt and water these wrappers are used to make dumplings. They can be bought fresh or frozen from any Chinese supermarket.

Wood ear mushrooms – *see* Chinese wood ear mushrooms

Yellow bean sauce (sauce)
This is made from fermented yellow soya beans, dark brown sugar and rice wine. It makes a great marinade for meats and as a flavouring in many savoury dishes.

Index

appetisers 38–73
asparagus and egg fried rice 186
aubergine:
    fish-fragrant with dofu 152, *153*
    fish-fragrant with pork *114*, 115
avocado, fried eggs and soy sauce,
    toast with 18, *19*

bacon lardons, shittake mushrooms
    and chestnuts, red-cooked 112, *113*
bamboo shoots 229
    in chilli oil, pickled 232
banana toffee fritters *214,* 215
basil:
    omelette with spicy sweet chilli
        sauce 20
    Victoria plums and heirloom
        tomatoes with sweet basil and
        salted plum shavings 63
basmati rice 229
bean curd 46, *47*, 152, *153*, 230, 231,
    234 *see also* dofu
bean paste, chilli 229
bean sprout:
    black bean wok-fried ribs with chillies
        and 110, *111*
beef:
    with bean sprouts and spring onions
        102, *103*
    black pepper and rainbow vegetable
        stir-fry 104, *105*
    chilli bean braised with coriander and
        steamed mantou 162, *163*
    chilli peanut 101
    curry in a hurry, Xi'an-style *106*, 107
    in oyster sauce with choy sum 100
    pancakes, crispy sweet chilli *56*, 57
beef, pork and lamb 96–117
berries, goji 231
big bowl of oat congee and
    accompaniments – 'The Works' *24*, 25
black bean 229
    and chicken stir-fry 79
    fermented salted 231
    mussels 122
    Oriental mushrooms with 150
    plaice steamed with *138*, 139
    wok-fried ribs with bean sprouts and
        chillies 110, *111*

black pepper beef and rainbow
    vegetable stir-fry 104, *105*
black rice vinegar 229, 230
boiled jasmine rice 184
breadcrumbs, panko 232
breaded mackerel with Sichuan
    pepper, chilli and salt 134
breakfast 15–25
Buddha's stir-fried mixed vegetables
    156
buns, roast pork brioche buns with
    caramelised red onions 172, *173*
buying and caring for your wok 223

Cantonese-style:
    roast duck and cucumber slices with
        salt and pepper 68, *69*
    roast duck with mango salad and
        plum dressing *70*, 71
    steamed lobster with ginger soy
        sauce 176, *177*
    sweet and sour pork 108
cassia bark 229
celery and dofu gan salad with sesame
    dressing 61
century eggs 229
Char sui roast pork noodle soup 198,
    199
chestnuts, water 234
chicken:
    and black bean stir-fry 79
    and cashew nuts, chilli 93
    with Chinese mushroom, goji berries
        and dried lily bulbs, steamed 85
    chow mein 197
    and duck 74–95
    General Tso's 80, *81*
    Hoisin *88*, 89
    King Po 82, *83*
    oyster-sauce with ginger and shittake
        mushrooms 86, *87*
    Sichuan chilli tomato 84
    skewers, fried sweet chilli 60
    three-cup 92
    twice-cooked salt and pepper 90, *91*
    yellow bean with French beans and
        shittake mushrooms 78
chilli:
    bean braised beef with coriander
        and steamed mantou 162, *163*
    bean paste 229
    chicken and cashew nuts 93
    crayfish tails and mango lettuce
        wraps 66, *67*
    dried Sichuan 233
    flakes, dried 230
    fried sweet chilli chicken skewers 60

oil 229
    peanut beef 101
    sauce 20, 229
Chinese cleaver/good knife 227
Chinese five spice 50, *51*, 229
Chinese fruity roast duck and wild rice
    salad 190
Chinese spatula/wooden spoon 227
Chinese sweet pork sausages with
    garlic 167
Chinese wood ear mushrooms 229–30
Chinese-style soft-shell crabs 54
Ching's life-changing Taiwanese liang
    mein 186
Ching's Yangzhou fried rice 188, *189*
Ching's zha jiang noodles 201
Chinkiang black rice vinegar 230
chow mein:
    chicken 197
    with pak choy, prawn and yellow
        bean 202, *203*
choy sum 230
    beef in oyster sauce with 100
    with oyster sauce, light 151
cinnamon stick/bark 230
clams:
    and Chinese sausage with bean
        sprouts and spring onions 178, *179*
    mushroom and ginger wined 132, *133*
classic plain congee 191
cleaver, Chinese 227
cloves 230
cold sesame prawns and cucumber 65
congee 230
    classic plain 191
    pork, ginger and duck egg 23
coriander 230
    beef, chilli bean braised with
        steamed mantou and 162, *163*
    hot sauce 50, *51*
    and pickled onion salad, spiced 175
    pickled whole radishes with 64
    pork rib, turnip and carrot broth with
        34, *35*
    salad 175
crab:
    Chinese-style soft-shell 54
    and crayfish tail sweetcorn soup,
        posh 36
crackling pork shoulder with Chinese
    spices 164, *165*
crayfish:
    sweet chilli noodles 204, *205*
    tail and crab sweetcorn soup, posh 36
    tails and mango lettuce wraps, chilli
        66, *67*
crispy seaweed 44

crispy sweet chilli beef pancakes 56, 57
Cumberland sausage, green pepper
    and tomato fried rice with pineapple
    22
cumin 230
curry:
    powder 230
    Xi'an-style beef in a hurry 106, 107
cutting board 227

daikon or white radish 230
dark soy sauce 230
dates (dried), red 233
deep-fried dofu (bean curd) 230
deep frying 226
dessert 206–21
dofu (bean curd) 230
    deep-fried 230
    fish-fragrant aubergine with 152, 153
    with kimchi, 'stinky'-style aromatic
        46, 47
    ru 230
dou miao with enoki mushrooms 148,
    149
dried chilli flakes 230
dried Chinese mushrooms 230
dried shrimps 230
duck:
    Cantonese-style roast and cucumber
        slices with salt and pepper 68, 69
    Cantonese-style roast with mango
        salad and plum dressing 70, 71
    Chinese fruity roast and wild rice
        salad 190
    fruity sweet and sour 94, 95
    mock and tenderstem broccoli stir-
        fry 157

egg:
    century 229
    fried rice, asparagus and 186
    fried rice, smoked salmon and 21
    noodles 231
enoki mushrooms 231
    dou miao with 148, 149
equipment 221–7, 221, 228

fennel seeds 231
fermented bean curd 231
fermented salted black beans 231
fish:
    floss 231
    -fragrant aubergine with dofu 152, 153
    -fragrant aubergine with pork 114, 115
    sauce (nam pla) (condiment) 231
fish & shellfish 118–19

five spice:
    Chinese 229, 231
    salted prawns with hot coriander
        sauce 50, 51
floss, fish 231
flour:
    glutinous rice 231
    potato 233
fragrant star anise rice 184
French beans, yellow bean chicken with
    shiitake mushrooms and 78
fried rice:
    Ching's Yangzhou 188, 189
    egg 21, 186
    green pepper and tomato 22
fried sweet chilli chicken skewers 60
fritters, banana toffee 214, 215
fruity sweet and sour duck 94, 95
frying, deep 226

General Tso's chicken 80, 81
ginger and mushroom wined clams
    132, 133
glossary 229–34
glutinous rice 231
goji berries 231
garam masala 231
green beans, sesame 62
groundnut oil 231

Hakka-style pork belly 168, 169
halibut with lemon sauce, Japanese-
    style crispy 52, 53
hamburgers, ('tiger bites pig'), Chinese
    with pickled cucumber 170, 171
healthy sweet and sour king prawn
    stir-fry 126
heirloom tomatoes with sweet basil
    and salted plum shavings, Victoria
    plums and 63
hoisin:
    chicken 88, 89
    sauce 88, 89, 231

ice cream with exotic fruit, mango 217

Japanese-style crispy halibut with
    lemon sauce 52, 53
jasmine rice 231

kimchi 232
king po chicken 82, 83
king prawns in chilli tomato sauce with
    courgettes 127
knife 227

ladle 227
lamb:
    chops with pickled onion and
        coriander salad, spiced 174, 175
    stew, spicy 116, 117
liang mein, Ching's life-changing
    Taiwanese 186
light choy sum with oyster sauce 151
Ligusticum wallichii (herb/dried) 232
lily bulbs 232
lobster, Cantonese-style steamed with
    ginger soy sauce 176, 177
lotus root salad 145
lychee 232

mackerel, breaded with Sichuan
    pepper, chilli and salt 134
mango:
    and coconut pudding with orange
        cinnamon syrup 210, 211
    ice cream with exotic fruit 217
    salad and plum dressing,
        Cantonese-style roast duck with
        70, 71
mantou 232
    beef, chilli bean braised with
        coriander and steamed 162, 163
matrimony vine 23
miso paste 232
mock duck and tenderstem broccoli
    stir-fry 157
momoya 232
mu shu pork 72, 73
Mum's herbal soup 37
mung bean noodles (dried) 232
    vermicelli 234
mushroom:
    with black bean sauce, oriental 150
    Chinese wood ear 229–30
    dried Chinese 230
    enoki 231
    and ginger wined clams 132, 133
    oyster 232
    shimeji 233
    shiitake 233
    wood ear 234
mussels, black-bean 122

Nian gao 220–1, 221
noodles 192–205
    Ching's zha jiang 201
    crayfish sweet chilli 204, 205
    egg 231
    mung bean 232
    shi wheat-flour 233
    Singapore 200
    udon 234

vermicelli mung bean 234
wheat-flour flat udon 234
nutty prawn, asparagus and cashew
   nut stir-fry 123

oat congee and accompaniments -
   'The Works', big bowl of 24, 25
oil:
   chilli 229, 232
   groundnut 231
   sesame 233
   sesame toasted 234
omelette, basil with spicy sweet chilli
   sauce 20
oriental mushrooms with black bean
   sauce 150
oyster:
   mushrooms 232
   sauce 86, 87, 100, 151, 232
   sauce chicken with ginger and
      shittake mushrooms 86, 87

pak choy 232
   with carrot and garlic 144
   prawn and yellow bean chow mein
      with 202, 203
   XO sauce and pak choy squid 130,
      131
   yellow bean and prawn chow mein
      with 202, 203
pancakes:
   crispy sweet chilli beef 56, 57
   wheat-flour 234
panko breadcrumbs 232
paste, sesame 233
peppercorns, Sichuan 233–4
pickled bamboo shoots in chilli oil 232
pickled salad 151
pickled soy lettuce stems (preserve)
   232–3
pickled whole radishes with coriander
   64
pineapple and mango crunch trifle 216
plaice with black beans, steamed 138,
   139
plum:
   apple and lychee spring rolls in
      cinnamon sugar 212, 213
   and heirloom tomatoes with sweet
      basil and salted plum shavings,
      Victoria 63
   preserved salted 233
pork:
   belly, Hakka-style 168, 169
   brioche buns with caramelised red
      onions, roast 172, 173
   Cantonese-style sweet and sour 108

fillet with kimchi and enoki
   mushrooms 166
fish-fragrant aubergine with 114, 115
floss 233
ginger and duck egg congee 23
mu shu 72, 73
mushroom and ginger wontons,
   watercress soup with 32, 33
noodle soup, Char sui roast 198, 199
and prawn fried wontons 58, 59
rib, turnip and carrot broth with
   coriander 34, 35
salad, yin and yang crispy 109
sausages, Chinese sweet with garlic
   167
shoulder with Chinese spices,
   crackling 164, 165
posh crab and crayfish tail sweetcorn
   soup 36
potato flour 233
prawn:
   in chilli tomato sauce with
      courgettes, king 127
   five-spice salted with hot coriander
      sauce 50, 51
   healthy sweet and sour king stir-fry
      126
   nutty, asparagus and cashew nut
      stir-fry 123
   and pork fried wontons 58, 59
   spicy sweet king 124, 125
   toast, sesame 45
   and yellow bean chow mein with pak
      choy 202, 203
   with yellow bean sauce and garlic
      spinach, steamed giant
      Madagascar 128, 129
preserved mustard greens/pickled
   Chinese cabbage (preserved) 233
preserved salted plums 233
pudding with orange cinnamon syrup,
   mango and coconut 210, 211

radishes with coriander, pickled whole
   64
red dates (dried) 233
red-cooked bacon lardons, shittake
   mushrooms and chestnuts 112, 113
rehmannia (herb/dried), rhizome of
   233
rhizome of rehmannia (herb/dried) 233
ribs:
   black bean wok-fried with bean
      sprouts and chillies 110, 111
   pork rib, turnip and carrot broth with
      coriander 34, 35
   sweet and sour Wuxi 55

rice 180–91
   basmati 229
   boiled jasmine 184
   flour, glutinous 231
   fragrant star anise 184
   glutinous 231
   jasmine 231
   vinegar 233
   wine, Shaohsing 233
roast pork brioche buns with
   caramelised red onions 172, 173

salad:
   celery and dofu gan with sesame
      dressing 61
   Chinese fruity roast duck and wild
      rice 190
   lotus root 145
   mango salad and plum dressing 70,
      71
   pickled 151
   yin and yang crispy pork 109
   zesty fruit salad with star anise syrup
      218, 219
salmon and egg fried rice, smoked 21
sauce:
   black bean 150
   chilli 20, 127, 229
   coriander hot 50, 51
   dark soy 230
   fish 231
   ginger soy 176, 177
   Hoisin 231
   oyster 86, 87, 100, 151, 232
   spinach 136
   soy 18, 19, 176, 177, 230, 232
   yellow bean 18, 19, 128, 129
   XO 130, 131
sausage:
   Chinese sweet pork sausages with
      garlic 167
   clams and Chinese with bean
      sprouts and spring onions 178, 179
   Cumberland, green pepper and
      tomato fried rice with pineapple 22
sea bass
   with ginger and mushrooms,
      steamed 135
   in spinach sauce, steamed 136
seaweed, crispy 44
seeds, sesame 233
sesame:
   green beans 62
   oil 233, 234
   paste 233
   prawn toast 45
   prawns and cucumber, cold 65

seeds 233
spinach, yellow bean 147
Shaohsing rice wine 233
shellfish & fish 118–39
shi wheat-flour noodles (dried) 233
shimeji mushrooms 233
shittake mushrooms 233
　bacon lardons, and chestnuts, red-cooked 112, *113*
　yellow bean chicken with French beans and 78
shrimps, dried 230
Sichuan:
　chilli tomato chicken 84
　chillies/dried chilli flakes 233
　peppercorns 233–4
　preserved vegetables 234
　salt and pepper squid *48, 49*
Singapore noodles 200
smoked salmon and egg fried rice 21
snake beans 234
soup:
　Char sui roast pork noodle 198, *199*
　Mum's herbal 37
　posh crab and crayfish tail sweetcorn 36
　tomato and egg flower 30
　traditional hot and sour 31
　watercress with pork, mushroom and ginger wontons 32, *33*
soups 26–37
soy lettuce stems, pickled 232–3
soy sauce:
　dark 230
　light 232
special mixed vegetables *154, 155*
specials 158–79
spiced lamb chops with pickled onion and coriander salad *174, 175*
spicy lamb stew 116, *117*
spicy sweet king prawns 124, *125*
spinach, yellow bean sesame 147
spoon, Chinese spatula/wooden 227
spring roll:
　(chun juen), vegetable 42–3
　in cinnamon sugar, plum, apple and lychee 212, *213*
　wrappers/pastry 234
squid, Sichuan salt and pepper *48, 49*
star anise 234
　rice, fragrant 184
　zesty fruit salad with star anise syrup 218, *219*
starch, wheat 234
steamed chicken with Chinese mushroom, goji berries and dried lily bulbs 85

steamed giant Madagascar prawns with yellow bean sauce and garlic spinach 128, *129*
steamed plaice with black beans *138*, 139
steamed sea bass:
　with ginger and mushrooms 135
　in spinach sauce 136
steaming 228
stews, spicy lamb 116, *117*
'stinky' - style aromatic dofu with kimchi 46, *47*
stir-fry: 233–5
　bean sprout and spring onion 144
　black bean and chicken 79
　black pepper beef and rainbow vegetable 104, *105*
　healthy sweet and sour king prawn 126
　mixed vegetables, Buddha's 156
　nutty prawn, asparagus and cashew 123
　tenderstem broccoli and mock duck 157
sweet and sour:
　duck, fruity 94, *95*
　Wuxi ribs 55
sweet roasted vegetables 146

Taiwanese liang mein, Ching's life-changing 186
techniques for cooking in a wok 223–6
three-cup chicken 92
'tiger bites pig' (Chinese hamburgers) with pickled cucumber *170*, 171
toast with avocado, fried eggs and soy sauce 18, *19*
toasted sesame oil 234
toffee banana fritters *214, 215*
tofu 234
tomato:
　chicken, Sichuan chilli tomato 84
　Cumberland sausage, green pepper and tomato fried rice with pineapple 22
　and egg flower soup 30
　king prawns in chilli tomato sauce with courgettes 127
　Victoria plums and heirloom tomatoes with sweet basil and salted plum shavings 63
traditional hot and sour soup 31
trifle, pineapple and mango crunch 216
turmeric 234
twice-cooked salt and pepper chicken 90, *91*

udon noodles 234

vegetable:
　Buddha's stir-fried mixed 156
　Sichuan preserved 234
　special mixed *154*, 155
　spring rolls (chun juen) 42–3
　stir-fry, black pepper beef and rainbow 104, *105*
　sweet roasted 146
vegetarian 142–57
vermicelli mung bean noodles 234
Victoria plums and heirloom tomatoes with sweet basil and salted plum shavings 63
vinegar:
　black rice 229
　Chinkiang black rice 230
　rice 233

water chestnuts 234
watercress soup with pork, mushroom and ginger wontons 32, *33*
wheat starch 234
wheat-flour:
　flat udon noodles 234
　pancakes 234
white radish 230
wine, Shaohsing rice 233
wok 221
　buying and caring for your 223
　cover 227
wonton:
　pork, mushroom and ginger, watercress soup with 32, *33*
　prawn and pork fried 58, *59*
　wrappers 234
wood ear mushrooms 234
'The Works' 24, 25
Wuxi ribs, sweet and sour 55

Xi'an-style beef curry in a hurry *106*, 107
XO sauce and pak choy squid 130, *131*

yellow bean:
　chicken with French beans and shittake mushrooms 78
　and prawn chow mein with pak choy 202, *203*
　sauce 234
　sesame spinach 147
yin and yang crispy pork salad 109

zesty fruit salad with star anise syrup 218, *219*

Acknowledgements

I owe a huge thank you to all the cooks who have supported me throughout my career. It warms my heart whenever I receive a friendly kind message of love and support and it gives me great confidence and joy; I dedicate this book to you all. I hope this book will come in handy in the kitchen and give you more happy days of wokking to come. I also share some more of my stories with you.

From my very first beginnings on Great Food Live on the Good Food Channel, I owe another big thank you to Fiona Cho who helped me as a true friend, who believed in what I could achieve and allowed me to realise my dream and potential. I would not be where I am without your burst of inspiration and enthusiasm all those years ago. I am forever grateful.

Thank you to Toby Eady and everyone at Toby Eady Associates – Jamie Coleman, Zaria Rich and Nicole – for your unconditional love and support, and for continuing to champion me! To Michael Foster, Alexandra Henderson and Katie Rice at PFD who have helped me so much in the last year through some difficult times, thank you for all your hard work and belief.

This book would not have been possible without the special help and support of so many people. I would like to thank you from my heart for giving me this amazing opportunity to continue to do what I love – Victoria Barnsley, Belinda Budge, my (incredibly smart and beautiful) publisher Carole Tonkinson, my project editor Georgina Atsiaris and copyeditor Kate Parker, cover designer Richard Augustus and layout designer Sophie Martin. Thank you also to Liate Stehlik, Cassie Jones and everyone at HarperCollins US for making my dream come true.

Thanks to Jennifer Joel and Michael Kagan at ICM Talent in the US for helping to open up opportunities for me and for believing in me. Thank you for your incredible patience. Thanks to Tybalt Whitney – I have learned a lot from you!

To all my family, Buddhist masters, friends, fans, cooks and chefs who have helped me on my journey, past and present, I am indebted and ever grateful – special mentions to Sir David Tang KBE, Alan Yao OBE, Wing Yip OBE and David Mulcahy, Vice President of Craft Guild of Chefs, Holland and Andy Kwok of Good Earth Reastaurant and Jayne Hibbit.

Thanks to all the powers at Good Food Channel, BBC, Channel 5 and Cooking Channel (Bruce Seidel, Michael Smith), and the producers at Lion TV (Richard Shaw), Blink TV (Dan Chambers) and Optomen TV for continuing to give me opportunities and allowing me to share my cooking!

To Jamie – I can't believe we did this book together! This book will always be special to me because we both slaved over it – a labour of love, with me cooking every dish and you capturing it. However imperfect, it is perfect; thank you from my heart.

To Choi sum and Paco, I love your cankering and ankle-nipping antics when I'm washing up; thank you for your unconditional cuteness and love!